Foreword
<u>From Director Tessa Walker</u>

The Whip Hand is a rich, detailed and taut play that brilliantly works on many levels. It's a play full of humour and depth and darkness as what should be a joyous family celebration, quickly, darkly and devastatingly moves completely beyond a family's control, as they are forced to face up to their pasts, their responsibilities and each other, in a way none of them could have imagined.

The play manages to be about the fractures in one very specific family and simultaneously the state of a country. It also examines what responsibility any of us should really have to our individual and collective pasts, and asks what paying reparation really means. As heartfelt and as funny as it is moving and unsettling, it asks huge questions about loyalty, truth and family, and takes the audience on an extraordinary and unexpected journey.

It's a real privilege to be able to bring this play to life, particularly with the Birmingham Rep and the Traverse who both have such an honest and heartfelt commitment to new plays, new stories and new ways of seeing the world. That it sits in such a strong Traverse programme, at the heart of one of the biggest arts festivals in the world is even more thrilling.

Company Biographies

Michael Abubakar (Aaron)
Theatre includes: *Cadaver Police in the Electrocution Afterlife* (Tron Theatre); *Invisible Army* (Terra Incognita); *Dream On* (BBC Arts); *Romeo & Juliet, Death of A Salesman, Ghosts* (Royal Conservatoire of Scotland); *Blood Lines* (The Arches); *Der Rosenkavalier* (Scottish Opera).
TV includes: *TRUST ME* (Red Production Company LTD).

Iain Armstrong (Sound Designer)
Iain Armstrong is a composer and sound designer based in Birmingham, UK. He is particularly interested in exploring the creative potential of recordings of the sound environment and encouraging people to engage in, and enjoy, the act of listening. His work is presented internationally and spans sound design for theatre and dance, electronic music, multi-channel sound installation, photography and live electroacoustic performance. Recent work includes music composition for Humanhood's *ZERO* (mac Birmingham) and *Orbis* (Without Walls). Sound design for *Heather* by Thomas Eccleshare (Bush Theatre and Tobacco Factory Theatres); *Looking For John* by Tony Timberlake, *Stories to Tell In The Middle of the Night* by Francesca Millican-Slater (Birmingham Repertory Theatre); *The Twelfth Battle of Isonzo* and *Judith: A Parting from The Body* (Arcola Theatre, London); *Heartbeats & Algorithms* by Jenny Lee (Soho Theatre, London); *A Journey Round My Skull* (KILN Ensemble); *A Journey Round My Theatre*, an architectural soundwalk located in Birmingham Repertory Theatre; and upcoming *Delightful* (Birmingham Repertory Theatre).

Simon Bond (Lighting Designer)
Simon is a Lighting Technician at Birmingham Repertory Theatre.
Lighting designs for Birmingham Repertory Theatre include: *To Sir, With Love, Looking For John, The Quiet House, Rotters' Club, Of Mice And Men, Never Try This At Home, Finger Trigger Bullet Gun, Circles, Come Heavy Sleep, Hopelessly Devoted, The Legend of Mike Smith, Europa, Wounded, Hip Hope Hero, Cling To Me Like Ivy, Gravity, Looking For Yoghurt, The Just Price Of Flowers* and *Notes To Future Self.*
Further theatre credits: *Mary Queen of Scots Got Her Head Chopped Off, Punk Rock, The Misanthrope, Duchess Of Malfi, Cloud 9, Hayfever, Dracula* and *Hedda Gabler* (Birmingham School of Acting); *A Midsummer Night's Dream* and *As You Like It* (Custom Practice); *White Open Spaces* and *Strawberry Fields* (Pentabus Theatre).

Richard Conlon (Lorenzo)
Richard trained at Queen Margaret University College.
Recent theatre credits include: *God of Carnage, Harold &
Maude* (Tron Theatre); *Jumpy, The Iliad* and *The Crucible*
(Royal Lyceum Theatre Edinburgh); *Fat Alice* (Òran Mór);
Propaganda Swing (Nottingham Playhouse & Coventry
Belgrade); *Woman in Mind* (Dundee Rep/Birmingham
Repertory Theatre); *And Then There Were None* (Dundee
Rep); *Macbeth* (Perth Theatre); *Ane Pleasant Satyre of
the Thrie Estaitis* (ABandC Theatre); *Smalltown* (Random
Accomplice); *A View From The Bridge, The Merchant of
Venice, A Christmas Carol* and *As You Like It* (Royal Lyceum
Theatre Edinburgh); *Zorro* and *Peter Pan* (Visible Fictions);
Great Expectations (Prime Productions); *Brightwater* (Mull
Theatre); *Macbeth* (National Theatre of Scotland's Elgin
Project); *Cat on A Hot Tin Roof, The Glass Menagerie* and
Woman in Black (Byre Theatre). Richard was also an original
member of Dundee Rep Ensemble.
Richard's television and film credits include: *Garrow's Law*
(Shed Media/BBC); *Low Winter Sun* (Channel 4); *Age of
Genius* (BBC); *The Strange Case of Sherlock Holmes and
Arthur Conan Doyle* (BBC); *High Road* (ITV); *Taggart* (ITV)
and *Bad Boys* (BBC).
Various radio credits with BBC Radio 4.

Alison de Burgh (Fight Director)
Theatre includes: *The Tempest/Othello* (Stafford Festival);
King Lear (ATG); *How The Other Half Loves* (Theatre Royal,
Haymarket); *Twelfth Night/Anna Karenina* (Royal Exchange
Theatre, Manchester); *Posh* (Nottingham Playhouse); *A View
From the Bridge/The Scotsboro Boys, The Changeling*
(Young Vic); *A Little Hotel On The Side* (Theatre Royal, Bath);
The Ladykillers/Macbeth (Lyric Theatre, Belfast); *What The
Butler Saw, The Ladykillers, Private Lives, Speaking In
Tongues, The Dumb Waiter, Peter Pan, Bent, The Play's
The Thing, Donkey's Years, The Anniversary, As You Like
It* (London West End); *A Small Family Business, The Black
Album, Harper Regan, Therese Raquin, Coram Boy, Pillars
of the Community, Tales from the Vienna Woods* (National
Theatre); *It's A Mad World My Masters, Romeo and Juliet,
The Penelopiad, As You Like It, A Midsummer Night's
Dream* (Royal Shakespeare Company); *Sons Without Fathers*
(Belgrade, Coventry/Arcola).

Opera includes: *The Barber of Seville, La Fanciulla Del West, Cavalleria Rusticana & Pagliacci* (Holland Park Opera); *Carousel* (Opera North); *Don Giovanni, Knight Crew, Euryanthe* (Glyndebourne Festival Opera); *Florentine Tragedy/Gianni Schicci* (Greek National Opera); *Varjak Paw* (The Opera Group); *The Trojans at Carthage; The Handmaid's Tale; Lulu, Morning to Midnight* (English National Opera).

Natasha Jenkins (Designer)
Natasha is a designer and director. She studied Theatre, Film and Television at the University of Glasgow.
Theatre design credits include: *Monstrous Bodies* (Dundee Rep); *LOVE* (National Theatre/Birmingham Repertory Theatre); *20b* (Birmingham Repertory Theatre); *Beyond Caring* (National Theatre/The Yard); *How Was It For You?* (Unicorn Theatre); *Glengarry Glen Ross* (G12).
Short film design credits include: *Forgiveness* by Conor O'Callaghan; *Black Sheep* by Parminder Sandhu; *Loose Ends* by Natalie Burt (shortlisted for the East End Film Festival); *Latitude Project* by Jack Lowe; *Here We Are* by Pamela Carter.
Directing credits include: *1001 Nights* (Queens Theatre, Hornchurch/Tour). Assistant director credits include: *Beyond Caring* (The Yard); *The Table* (NT Studio); *Tonight at 8.30* (ETT); *Liar Liar* (Unicorn Theatre); *The Only True History of Lizzie Finn* (Southwark Playhouse); *1001 Nights* (Unicorn Theatre). Dramaturg credits include: *No Weddings Nor a Funeral* (RADA Festival); *20b* (Birmingham Repertory Theatre).
Natasha previously worked as a stage manager for companies including National Theatre, Young Vic, West End, Almeida, Royal Court, Unicorn and Tramway.

Louise Ludgate (Arlene)
Louise trained at the Royal Scottish Academy of Music and Drama.
Theatre credits include: *Lanark* (Citizens Theatre/Edinburgh International Festival); *Home, The House of Bernada Alba, Realism, Little Otik* (National Theatre of Scotland); *Mainstream, Casanova, Lament* (Suspect Culture); *Greta, Sex and Drugs* (Traverse Theatre); *Iron* (Traverse Theatre/ Royal Court); *The Adoption Papers, Strawgirl* (Royal Exchange Theatre); *Cities of the Blind, Home Hinderance* (Fire Exit); *SubRosa* (Fire Exit/Citizens Theatre); *Dig* (Paines Plough); *Jeff Koons* (Actors Touring Company); *Balgay Hill*

(Dundee Rep); *13 Sunken Years* (Stellar Quines/Lung Ha); *Sex and God* (Magnetic North); *Shattered Head* (Òran Mór/Traverse Theatre); *Slice* (Gilded Ballon/Òran Mór); *World Domination* (Sherman Theatre/Òran Mór); *Thank You, Guilty, Resurrection, Out on the Wing, Midge Burgers, The Golden Silence, Moon Walking, Wired, The Date, Days of Wine, Rosie, The Gun, Rumplestiltskin, Fishwrap* (Òran Mór); *Total Strangers, Blackden* (Tron Theatre); *The Crucible, The Devils, The Wedding* (The Arches); *The Hanging Tree* (Lookout). Film and TV work includes: *Spooks, River City, Romance Class, Freedom, The Key, Sea of Souls, Glasgow Kiss* (BBC); *High Times, Taggart* (ITV); *Swung* (Sigma Films); *The Elemental* (Northlight); *Night People* (Newfoundland Films). Various radio credits with BBC.

Douglas Maxwell (Writer)
Douglas Maxwell has been one of Scotland's top playwrights since his debut in 2000. His recent work includes *Yer Granny* (a version of Roberto Cossa's *La Nona*) for the National Theatre of Scotland, *Fever Dream: Southside* for Citizens Theatre, Glasgow and *Charlie Sonata* for the Royal Lyceum Theatre, Edinburgh.
His many other plays include *Decky Does a Bronco, Mancub, Promises Promises* (staged in New York as *The Promise*) and *A Respectable Widow Takes to Vulgarity*.
His plays have been performed in Germany, Norway, Hong Kong, New York, Chicago, Holland, Canada, Sweden, New Zealand, Wales, Japan, France, Belgium and South Korea, where his debut play *Our Bad Magnet* has run for over ten years.
His plays are published by Oberon books. His first collection of work focuses on his writing for younger audiences. As well as *Decky Does a Bronco* and *Mancub*, the volume also contains *Too Fast, The Mother Ship* and *Helmet*.
Douglas lives on the Southside of Glasgow with his wife and two daughters.

Joanne Thomson (Molly)
Joanne is a graduate of the Royal Conservatoire of Scotland. Theatre credits include: *The Choir* (ATG/Citizens Theatre); *Kill Johnny Glendenning* (Royal Lyceum Theatre Edinburgh/ Citizens Theatre); *A Midsummer Night's Dream* (Bard in the Botanics); *Cinderella* (Qdos/King's Theatre Edinburgh); *Mwanawashe* (Ankur Productions/Tron Theatre); *Blackout* (ThickSkin); *The Breathing House, Anna Weiss* (Tron Theatre); *Theatre Uncut* (Traverse Theatre).

Credits in training include: *Festen* (Tron Theatre); *Macbeth*, *Miseryguts* and *Tartuffe* (Royal Conservatoire of Scotland). Film/TV credits include: *In Plain Sight* (ITV/World Productions); *WW1 Centenary Commemoration Service live* (BBC1); *The Creator* (Digicult/BFI); *BB* (Kate Burton Films); *Shieldinch Nights* (Royal Conservatoire of Scotland /BBC Scotland); *Wasteland 26* (Breaking Point Flix); *Adolescence* and *Sunsets & Silhouettes* (Factotum); *Scottish Government Breastfeeding Campaign* (MTP/STV).

Tessa Walker (Director)
Tessa is an Associate Director at Birmingham Repertory Theatre where she has directed *A Christmas Carol* adapted by Bryony Lavery, *The Mother* adapted by Mark Ravenhill, *Circles* by Rachel De-Lahay, *Back Down* by Steven Camden, *The Lion, the Witch and the Wardrobe* adapted by Adrian Mitchell, *Folk* by Tom Wells, *The Quiet House* by Gareth Farr and *Looking for John* by Tony Timberlake.
Other directing includes: *The Gatekeeper* by Chloe Moss (Royal Exchange Theatre, Manchester), *The Glee Club* by Richard Cameron (Hull Truck), *The Company Will Overlook a Moment of Madness* adapted by Morna Pearson (National Theatre of Scotland), *Dream Pill* by Rebecca Prichard and *Dancing Bears* by Sam Holcroft (Soho Theatre), *The Red Helicopter* by Robin French (Almeida Theatre), *She From the Sea* by Zawe Ashton (LIFT), *Harm's Way* by Zawe Ashton (The Lowry, Manchester), *Black Crows* by Linda Brogan (Arcola Theatre), *Orange* by Alan Harris (Script Cymru), *Debris* by Dennis Kelly (Theatre 503, BAC Critics' Choice Season, Traverse Theatre and Staatstheater Biennale, Germany).
She has also been Literary Director at Paines Plough and Literary Associate at the National Theatre of Scotland.

Jonathan Watson (Dougie)
Born in Glasgow, Jonathan trained at the Royal Scottish Academy of Music and Drama. On leaving college he joined the Glasgow Citizens' TAG Theatre Company and went on to work with the Traverse Theatre, Borderline, 7:84, Royal Lyceum Theatre, Perth Theatre and the Scottish Theatre Company, while returning to the Citizens Theatre on many occasions.
Recent theatre work includes: Rob Drummond's *Quiz Show* (Traverse Theatre); John Byrne's adaptation of Chekhov's *The Three Sisters* (Tron Theatre); and Douglas Maxwell's *Yer Granny* (National Theatre of Scotland).

Film work includes: *Local Hero, Girl in the Picture, The Match, Solid Geometry, Filth* and the award-winning horror film *Let Us Prey*, which premiered at the Edinburgh International Film Festival.

Television work includes: *Naked Video, City Lights, Rab C. Nesbitt, The Bill, Casualty, New Town, Garrow's Law, New Tricks, Rubenesque, Mountain Men, Waterloo Road, Scotland in a Day, Fried, Upstart Crow, Bob Servant, Only an Excuse?* and *Two Doors Down*. Filming has just been completed on *Back* for Channel 4, and a third series of *Two Doors Down* starts recording soon for BBC2, including a Christmas special.

About Traverse Theatre Company

The Traverse is Scotland's new writing theatre.

Formed in 1963 by a group of passionate theatre enthusiasts, the Traverse was founded to extend the spirit of the Edinburgh festivals throughout the year. Today, under Artistic Director Orla O'Loughlin, the Traverse nurtures emerging talent, produces award-winning new plays and offers a curated programme of the best work from the UK and beyond, spanning theatre, dance, performance, music and spoken word.

The Traverse has launched the careers of some of the UK's most celebrated writers – David Greig, David Harrower and Zinnie Harris – and continues to discover and support new voices – Stef Smith, Morna Pearson, Gary McNair and Rob Drummond.

With two custom-built and versatile theatre spaces, the Traverse's home in Edinburgh's city centre is a powerhouse of vibrant new work for, and of, our time. Every August, it holds an iconic status as the theatrical heart of the Edinburgh Festival Fringe.

Outside the theatre walls, it runs an extensive engagement programme, offering audiences of all ages and backgrounds the opportunity to explore, create and develop. Further afield, the Traverse frequently tours internationally and engages in exchanges and partnerships – most recently in Quebec, New Zealand and South Korea.

'The Traverse remains the best new writing theatre in Britain.'
The Guardian

For more information about the Traverse please visit traverse.co.uk.

Traverse Theatre – The Company

About Birmingham Repertory Theatre

Birmingham Repertory Theatre Company is one of Britain's leading producing theatre companies. Its mission is to inspire a lifelong love of theatre in the diverse communities of Birmingham and beyond. As well as presenting over 60 productions on its three stages every year, the theatre tours its productions nationally and internationally, showcasing theatre made in Birmingham.

The commissioning and production of new work lies at the core of The REP's programme and over the last 15 years, the company has produced more than 130 new plays. The theatre's outreach programme engages with over 7000 young people and adults through its learning and participation programme, equating to 30,000 individual educational sessions. The REP is also committed to nurturing new talent through its youth theatre groups and training for up and coming writers, directors and artists through its REP Foundry initiative. The REP's Furnace programme unites established theatre practitioners with Birmingham's communities to make high quality, unique theatre.

Many of The REP's productions go on to have lives beyond Birmingham. Recent tours include *What Shadows*, *The Government Inspector*, *Of Mice And Men*, *Anita And Me*, *Back Down* and *The King's Speech*. The theatre's long-running production of *The Snowman* will celebrate its 20th anniversary at the Peacock Theatre, London this year as well as touring to Manchester, Glasgow, Southampton, Brighton and Milton Keynes.

Artistic Director Roxana Silbert
Executive Director Stuart Rogers

Box Office 0121 236 4455
birmingham-rep.co.uk

Birmingham Repertory Theatre is a registered charity (Reg Charity No: 223660).

Birmingham Repertory Theatre staff

REP Patrons
June Brown
Soweto Kinch
Josie Lawrence
Martin Shaw
David Suchet
Dame Janet Suzman
Mark Williams

Directors of Birmingham Repertory Theatre Limited
Johanne Clifton
Mark Goucher
Guy Hemington
Liz James
Cllr Narinder Kaur Kooner
Lorna Laidlaw
Greg Lowson
Angela Maxwell (Chair)
Paul Phedon
Prof. David Roberts
Amerah Saleh
Cllr Gary Sambrook
Grace Smith
Prof Michael Whitby

Executive Director
Stuart Rogers

Artistic Director
Roxana Silbert

Associate Directors
Steve Ball
Tessa Walker
Alexander Zeldin

Community Engagement Producer
Rosalyn Lesurf-Olner

Assistant Producer
Lynette Dakin

Stage One Assistant Producer
Catherine Fowles

Agent for Change
Billy Coughlin

Arts Team Administrator
Sarah-Katy Davies

Trainee Associate Director
Daniel Bailey

Associate Artists
Caroline Horton
KILN Ensemble
Paul O'Donnell
Amerah Saleh

Head of Education
Daniel Tyler

Learning & Participation Manager
Lauren Fallon

Education Officers
Mel Daly
Rebecca Deeks
Bhavik Parmar
Lucy Wild

Head of Youth Theatre
Tom Saunders

Youth Theatre Director
Philip Morris

Finance Director
Neil Harris

Financial Controller
Anne Russell

Finance Assistants
Sandra Bayliss
Margaret Evans
Claire Monk
Justyna Potrebko
Vidhu Sharma
Mashal Zahra

General Manager
Trina Jones

Head of Marketing & Communications
Paul Reece

PR Manager
Clare Jepson-Homer
0121 245 2072

Marketing Campaigns Manager
Richard Leigh

Marketing Communications Officer
Lucy Dwyer

Marketing & Digital Assistant
Victoria Ellery-Jones

Marketing & Fundraising Assistant
Victoire Mullet

Head of Fundraising
Rachel Cranny

Fundraising Officer
Emma Jackson

Commercial Director
Suzanna Reid

Events Co-ordinator
Sharon Bennett

Events Finance Administrator
Nova Smith

Events Manager
Erika Jarvis

Events Supervisors
Vanessa Bull
Agnieszka Skiba

Events Assistants
Deborah Boateng
Charlotte Dodd
Laura Grant
Natalie Herran
Somya Iqbal
Balazs Rozgonyi
Caroline Shephard
Aimee Sheriff
Jess Vantielcke

Theatre Sales Manager
Gerard Swift

Assistant Theatre & Sales Managers
Rachel Foster
Kieran Johnson

Theatre & Sales Assistants
Jess Clixby
Rachel Cooper
Hannah Kelly
Sebastian Maynard-Francis
Eileen Minnock
Rhys Worgan

Theatre Operations Manager
Nigel Cairns

Theatre Concierge
Andrew Daniels

Theatre Housekeeper
Jane Browning

Theatre Cleaning Assistants
Juliet Ayiku
Neville Claxton
Debra Cuthill
Ilyas Fareed
Emma Fowler
Tracey O'Dell
Ade Ogunbase
Beverley Shale

Head of Production
Tomas Wright

Production Manager
Milorad Žakula

Production Co-ordinator
Molly Taylor

Company Manager
Ruth Morgan

Head of Wardrobe
Kay Wilton

Cutter/Maker
Sue Nightingale

Head of Lighting
Andrew Fidgeon

Senior Technician (Lighting)
Simon Bond

Technician (Lighting)
Alex Boucher
Dermot Finnegan

Head of Sound & AV
Dan Hoole

Senior Technician (Sound & AV)
Clive Meldrum

Technician (Sound)
Andy Gregory

Head Scenic Artist
Christopher Tait

Head of Technical Design
Ebrahim Nazier

Head of Construction
Margaret Rees

Senior Scenic Maker
Neil Parkes

Scenic Makers
Ed Cartwright
Christopher Maggs

Technical Co-ordinator
Adrian Bradley

Technical Events Manager
Chris Ball

Senior Technician (Stages)
Ross Gallagher

Technician (Stages)
Oscar Turner

Senior Technician (Events)
Isaac Vivian

Building Maintenance Technician
Leon Gatenby

With thanks to all casual staff and volunteers

THE WHIP HAND

Douglas Maxwell

THE WHIP HAND

OBERON BOOKS
LONDON

WWW.OBERONBOOKS.COM

First published in 2017 by Oberon Books Ltd
521 Caledonian Road, London N7 9RH
Tel: +44 (0) 20 7607 3637 / Fax: +44 (0) 20 7607 3629
e-mail: info@oberonbooks.com
www.oberonbooks.com

PB ISBN: 9781786822420
E ISBN: 9781786822437

Cover image by Mihaela Bodlovic

Printed, bound and converted
by CPI Group (UK) Ltd, Croydon, CR0 4YY.

Visit www.oberonbooks.com to read more about all our books and to buy them. You will also find features, author interviews and news of any author events, and you can sign up for e-newsletters so that you're always first to hear about our new releases.

It's DOUGIE BELL's birthday. He's fifty years old. This is not his house.

This house is sleek...chic...substantial.

We're in the family room: leather L-shaped couch and wall-mounted flat screen; pieces of funky vintage décor sit alongside recognisable Ikea stuff; the framed prints are bold but familiar.

DOUGIE feels unsure here. Nervous. As visible as a tourist. So he's careful, quiet and smiling. He's wearing new clothes: a short-sleeved shirt, jeans and black leather shoes.

The house belongs to LORENZO and ARLENE. ARLENE is DOUGIE's ex-wife and the mother of his daughter, MOLLY. MOLLY has just left school. She goes to university after the summer.

Tonight's a wee celebration. Aren't we all good? We have survived the past and we have a wonderful future...

DOUGIE's struggling with a laptop and projector. He's trying to get PowerPoint going but it's not working. He's embarrassed and angry at himself.

He appeals to AARON for some assistance. AARON is his nephew – his sister's son – and he comes over to help. AARON is in his late teens/early twenties and seems as uptight about this PowerPoint thing as DOUGIE. AARON's trying to appear breezy and casual though – in fact his plan is to be breezy and casual all evening – but it's a tough sell. Every now and then we can see the strain on his face.

It's taken as read that AARON is on "DOUGIE's side". He's even dressed a little like him.

DOUGIE, ARLENE, LORENZO and MOLLY are white. AARON is mixed-race.

AARON taps away on the laptop like an expert and soon finds a problem. A very old black and white photograph is projected up onto the wall. The wrong photograph. DOUGIE's not happy. AARON waves him down... "I know, I know, give me a minute." AARON shakes his head, frustrated and a little panicked: Uncle DOUGIE's buggered this up already – what's he done?!

This photo is of a man called William "Saracen" Bell. We're going to be hearing a lot about Saracen Bell. We see an unsmiling, weather-beaten old hardcase; wild beard and a tough, grooved face. His eyes…his eyes… there's something about those eyes. Those eyes will give no quarter. They see a world that deserves nothing but hatred. He looks like a war-worn General from the American Civil War, but without the humanity of those men.

LORENZO comes in from the kitchen with two bottles of beer. He's younger than DOUGIE and wears it well. He's at ease. Always at ease. He's casual in worn jeans, Crocs and a creased shirt. He's a creative guy. He's good looking. He's always been lucky. DOUGIE tells everyone that LORENZO is one of the nicest people he's ever met.

LORENZO: Any joy?

DOUGIE: Oh eh…aye. Well, naw.

LORENZO: *(About the photo.)* Uh oh. Santa looks pissed off. Ha ha ha!

DOUGIE: *(Awkward.)* Aye, kinda…That one's meant to be last…it's…I was kinda going tae save it till folk get here and are all kinda….

LORENZO: Cool.

DOUGIE: But honestly, Lorenzo, I can just tell you now.

LORENZO: Nah, it's sweet.

DOUGIE: *(To LORENZO.)* I mean it's your house, I can just tell you now. If you want. I'll just tell you now.

LORENZO: I can wait Dougie, honestly. They won't be long.

AARON: *(At the laptop, to DOUGIE.)* What have you done to this, man? It was all set.

DOUGIE: Ach. Don't need it anyroads. Daft so it wis.

AARON: You've somehow manged to delete every single file bar one. How is that even possible?

DOUGIE: *(To LORENZO.)* I'll just tell you now then.

LORENZO: Chill man, they'll be two ticks. I can wait. *(Joking.)* But not for long! The suspense! My God the suspense!

AARON: *(Head still in the laptop.)* No trace of it. Gone. Unbelievable.

DOUGIE: *(Smiling nervously.)* Dunno what I've done. Daft, man. Maybe I've built it up too much or something?

LORENZO: I'm just gagging to know what's got you so excited.

DOUGIE: Everyone'll be excited. It's an exciting thing. Sure it is Aaron?

AARON: It is actually. Or it was.

LORENZO: Me and Arlene were saying last night, "Dougie's doing a *presentation*? Eh?!" It's the least "Dougie" thing ever!

DOUGIE: I shouldnae've called it a presentation. Daft man. Yous are right. Stupit. So it is.

LORENZO: It's good to see you buzzing.

DOUGIE: I'll just tell you now then.

LORENZO: Nooooo! It's *your* night, mate. You run the show. You said you were doing a wee presentation...

DOUGIE: Dunno why I said presentation. Built it up.

LORENZO: *(Cont.)* ...so a presentation we shall have.

AARON: *(Giving up.)* I suppose technically it's more of a speech now, rather than presentation. But it'll still work. I think. Should be fine. Just speak it.

DOUGIE: I'll just speak it.

LORENZO: *(About the laptop.)* I can have a look in a minute if you want?

AARON: Nah. That ship has sailed. Cheers though.

LORENZO: *(Handing a beer to DOUGIE.)* Right. Here you go birthday boy. Check this shit out.

DOUGIE: Uh huh. I brought beers but. So I did.

LORENZO: Have this one.

DOUGIE: Tennent's.

LORENZO: Have this one. It's a little brewery in the mountains right, cool as fuck. Cooks one batch of this nectar per year. Folk trek from Australia just for a taste. Go on, man.

DOUGIE sips it.

DOUGIE: Oh aye.

LORENZO: Get it?

DOUGIE: *(No.)* Uh huh.

LORENZO: Chocolate. And chilli. It's unreal right?

DOUGIE: Aye. God. So it is. Mental. Strong, but eh?

LORENZO: Totally organic though. No hangover. Ever. That other shit's a chemical compound man. You pay the next day let me tell you. *(To AARON. A little awkward this.)* Eh…I didn't know if you'd want one, Aaron. Or do you? I mean, you can.

AARON: *(He does want one but being polite.)* Em. Well…

LORENZO: I just thought, you know, what with…

AARON: Okay, aye. I'll try one. Thanks.

LORENZO: I mean we've loads of soft drinks and stuff.

DOUGIE: You've to take what he gives you Aaron.

AARON: He's not given me anything.

LORENZO: You could have a Coke or something?

DOUGIE: Aye, he'll have a Coke.

AARON: But if there's another one of those, I wouldn't say no.

DOUGIE: It's Lorenzo's house.

AARON: *(Taking the hint. Shrugging it off with a smile. Trying to be light…)* Oh of course. Aye. Absolutely. That's fine then. A Coke's fine Lorenzo. Thanks man. Honestly.

Beat.

LORENZO: Ach you know what. It's a special occasion. Have a beer. And if the thunder should fall from the mountain I'll just tell her, "Hey! It's his Uncle Dougie's big Five-Oh, give the guy a break". *(A voice.)* "Five-oh! Five-oh!" Get it Aaron? From *The Wire?*

AARON: Never seen it.

LORENZO: *(Playfully.)* Did I get away with the reference though? Politically speaking?

AARON: *(Smiling.)* See…Lorenzo…If you have to ask.

LORENZO: *(Laughs. Heading for the kitchen.)* Oh no! One beer on the way then. Suitable payment I hope for all my cringeworthy cultural appropriation!

AARON and LORENZO laugh.

DOUGIE didn't follow that last bit at all. He tries to smile but it ends up looking like a grimace.

There's the sound of the front door opening and people coming in from outside. Keys rattle, jackets are hung…

LORENZO stops in his tracks.

LORENZO: Uh oh. Officers on deck. Ten-shun!

MOLLY and ARLENE come in.

MOLLY is 18. She's fresh-faced, zesty and clever. Every teacher's favourite. You can tell from her smile that she's going to be fine. Her eyes sparkle with the promise of it all. She's wearing a brightly coloured uniform – polo shirt and shorts – from her summer job as a lifeguard and swimming coach at the local pool.

ARLENE is roughly the same age as DOUGIE and from the same background. She's wearing expensive heels, leather trousers and a patterned silk top. Loads of jewellery. It's on the very edge of too much. ARLENE is made of steel. It's her steel that built all of this. She sets the tone of every room she's in. The people at work respect her, but they tread carefully around her. She's aware of that, and it troubles her sometimes – why don't people love her? Or thank her? – but fuck it; what you gonna do? Right now she's all smiles. Tonight's a great night – it has been decided.

DOUGIE only has eyes for MOLLY.

AARON is noticeably awkward around ARLENE and vice versa, although she's very good at faking ease. There was an incident between them in the recent past and there's been no time since for them to talk it through. Their smiles say: "all is forgotten"; and, of course, simultaneously, exactly the opposite.

But at the moment, she and MOLLY have worked out a wee song for DOUGIE. They both sing…

MOLLY AND ARLENE: *(Singing.)* "Happy birthday to ya! Happy biiiirthday!!!"

DOUGIE: *(Playing along.)* Aw naw…singing.

MOLLY AND ARLENE: *(Singing.)* "Happy birthday to ya! Happy biiiirthday!!!"

Big laughs all round. MOLLY hugs DOUGIE.

DOUGIE: Thanks Molls. *(A rehearsed line.)* Yer old boy's getting old eh? Ha ha.

ARLENE: *(Kissing DOUGIE.)* Happy birthday Doogs. Fifty years old, eh? What a neck! Ach, don't worry, you'll always be a hot nineteen in my eyes, doll. *(To LORENZO.)* Right you. G&T or D.I.V.O.R.C.E. The decision is yours!

LORENZO: *(To ARLENE.)* G&T coming up. And a beer for Aaron.

ARLENE: A beer for Aaron?

LORENZO: Yeah, well. You know. Special occasion and all that.

ARLENE: No, that's fine.

LORENZO: Oh come on, one beer's not going to…

ARLENE: I'm saying it's fine.

AARON: Look, I can have a Coke or…

ARLENE: No, it's fine! Absolutely. Have a beer, darling! It's a celebration.

LORENZO rolls his eyes for AARON's benefit and exits off to the kitchen.

MOLLY: *(About the photo. Delighted.)* Oh my God! Is this your thing?

DOUGIE: Aye, but I cannae…it's no hingme. Started. That should be at the end but…know what I mean.

MOLLY: Aaron'll fix it for you.

DOUGIE: It's him that bloody done it.

AARON: Eh, excuse me! I pulled some graphics together and made the PowerPoint but I didn't lose all the bloody pictures. Nobody knows what happened with that. *(He points at DOUGIE and mouths "he fucked it".)*

MOLLY laughs. ARLENE's looking at the picture on the wall.

ARLENE: Right. I am sooooo intrigued by the way. Who's this? Tell-me-tell-me-tell-me!

DOUGIE: *(To MOLLY, dodging that.)* How was work the day?

MOLLY: Ach, Moira was off so I had eight kids in my section. It's too many, man. There's no teaching going on. All you can do is make sure none of the little mingers drown. Keeping children alive really wears you out. I'm like… dead or something.

DOUGIE: Go to bed if you want.

MOLLY: *(Laughing.)* What? No!

DOUGIE: Honest. I won't mind or anything.

ARLENE remembers something and shouts off to the kitchen…

ARLENE: Oh! Bring the cake in! Lorenzo! *(To DOUGIE.)* Don't start without me right? Lorenzo!

LORENZO hasn't heard, so ARLENE skips off to the kitchen.

MOLLY: *(Mock annoyed.)* And, eh, of *course* I'm not going to bed! It's my party too! Remember? Hello? Exam results? University in September? I'm the star!

AARON: *(At the laptop. About the photo.)* Off or on? I'm thinking keep it on. For the effect I mean?

DOUGIE: Naw. Daft now so it is. Switch it off.

MOLLY: No! I'm loving this guy! Keep him there. He's hypnotic.

DOUGIE: Still liking it then? The lifeguarding?

MOLLY: Meh. I stink of chlorine and it won't wash off.

DOUGIE: Got tae dae it but, eh? Save the sheckles?

MOLLY: Yeah. Well. Trying to.

DOUGIE: Good to have a summer job. So it is. Money in the bank.

MOLLY: Yeah. Suppose.

DOUGIE: And you can always get some work down there too eh? If you need any extra hingme. Folk'll snap you up, Molly doll, honest to God.

AARON: *(Teasing.)* You are the Golden Girl after all.

MOLLY: *(Happily playing along with AARON. Doing a pose…)* And don't you forget it wee man. I'm a desirable commodity in the marketplace and always will be. Unlike my poor unemployable cousin here.

AARON mimes a dagger in his heart – mortally wounded by that insult. They're playing.

ARLENE re-enters with the cake and a long kitchen knife. DOUGIE goes over. MOLLY and AARON don't even give it a glance.

ARLENE: Ta dah! Made it myself. Not really. Should've. Sorry doll. Work's been mental. It was bought with love though.

DOUGIE: Oh wow…

AARON: *(Still to MOLLY, playing. Mock offended.)* I don't know… she gets a couple of good exam results and suddenly she's dishing out the cheek to her elders and betters.

MOLLY: "Betters"? Aye right.

DOUGIE: *(Still about the cake.)* That is really beautiful. Don't know what to say.

MOLLY: Eh, and excuse me, but it wasn't just "a couple of good exam results". I got the full set so shut it!

ARLENE: Right now Molly shoosh. Aaron got two As.

MOLLY: I got *four* As. And a B.

AARON: Ah, but you're a genius though. To even compete with the Golden Girl would be foolishness in the extreme.

MOLLY: *(Laughs.)* Ha ha ha! Aw...I've missed having you round the place to torture, Cuz. *(Switching to a more genuine tone...)* And I miss our chats. Mum thinks talking about politics is a waste of time.

ARLENE: No, I think talking pish is a waste of time.

MOLLY: *(Still to AARON.)* Get that article I forwarded on? "Intersectional Feminism in the Age of Trump."

AARON: Em...

MOLLY: And there's a march next Saturday. Fancy it? No? *(Teasing again.)* Intimidated by my massive intellect? Don't worry I'll explain all the big words.

MOLLY laughs but AARON clouds over. He looks a little pained.

He's saved from having to respond though by ARLENE bulldozing in...

ARLENE: Ach leave him alone. Artists have lost years all the time, sure they do?

AARON: I'm not an artist though.

ARLENE: Aye but you could be, is what I'm saying. If you get stuck back into it. Or computing – which is just as creative as painting if you ask me. Ach now you know the right road to take. You've got everything clear in your head, sure you do? You'll amaze us all, Aaron. Anyday now. I can feel it. *(In a slightly different, jokier voice.)* And eh, by the way, muggins here was a late bloomer, so there ye go. I left school wi hee haw and check me noo. Social Worker To The Stars!

DOUGIE: Aye, but our school was shite. Sure it was?

ARLENE: Our school was fine. But see when I took control of my *emotional* education...which was when I was like, thirty or something by the way...well...it was night school and it was Open University and I couldnae get enough of the stuff. *(To DOUGIE.)* Transformed. Sure I was?

DOUGIE: Aye.

ARLENE: And then I was gone. Whoosh! Like a bird. So it's different for different folk, is what I'm saying. The right path might not be clear until later on, Aaron. Don't you panic.

AARON: Who's panicking?

DOUGIE: *(About AARON.)* Gave up on the sport an aw. That wis another disappointment.

AARON: Actually, for the record, sport gave up on me.

DOUGIE: Chucked it.

ARLENE gives AARON a big hug but it's a little forced. She's working hard to get a positive reaction from him. Too hard...

ARLENE: Right, could everyone please stop picking on my gorgeous nephew! If you're going for him you've to come through me, and I'm all about the love tonight so don't bother! *(A voice.)* I want to languish luxuriantly in the bosom of my wonderful family. *(A different voice.)* So nae rammying! And sorry for saying "bosom" there, Aaron. Has it set you off? Do you need to go to the bathroom?

ARLENE, MOLLY and AARON laugh. Although AARON's laugh might just be an attempt to end this little exchange. If so, it worked. He's released from the hug...

MOLLY: Mum!

ARLENE: Oh sorry darling, was that inappropriate? I forgot that your generation finds absolutely everything unacceptable. Touchy wee babies that you are. You getting changed?

MOLLY: Me? No. Why?

ARLENE: Ach. It's your work stuff. There'll be selfies later. C'mon, look nice. I've gone glam.

MOLLY: No, it's just us. I can't be bothered.

ARLENE: What about your hair though? Did you wash it when you came out the pool?

MOLLY: *(Childishly.)* Mum, I'm not changing! God sake!

ARLENE: Okay, okay. Whatever. *(Reluctantly letting it go. Change of subject. The photo…)* Right. Here we go then. The famous "birthday presentation"! Let's do this! Woo!

DOUGIE: Aye but no really. Shouldnae've said "presentation". That one was meant to be up last. Spoilt it man.

ARLENE: *(To AARON.)* Got to be fixable?

AARON: It'll still work without the visuals. I think. Should do anyway.

DOUGIE: Nah, it's bust. Daft to even bloody…ach, I dunno now.

AARON: *(Reassuring.)* It will work. Just…just do it. As planned.

LORENZO has entered, takes the G&T to ARLENE and gives AARON the beer.

LORENZO: Couldn't find the gin at first, but crisis averted.

ARLENE: *(About the laptop.)* It'll be all that porn you watch Dougie. Clogged up the pipes. Ha ha ha!

That's a sore one for DOUGIE. He hates ARLENE making cracks like that in front of MOLLY.

DOUGIE: I havenae even got a computer, Arlene. That's Aaron's.

ARLENE: Ooft! Christ that's worse! He crashed here for three weeks remember, and these walls are thin. I know what he's up to in that bedroom all day and it's got nothing to do with "intersectional feminism" I can tell you that. Ha ha ha!

AARON's not a fan of these gags either. He's stone faced.

LORENZO: *(To DOUGIE.)* You should get yourself an iPad, man. Or a Kindle Fire. That would be better for you actually. You can get them for about fifty quid.

DOUGIE: Em. *(With effort, but sincerely.)* Aye, I know. So I should Lorenzo. You're right. You're right. I should just bloody get one. I dunno though.

LORENZO: *(About the laptop.)* Want me to take a peep under the hood?

AARON: No.

DOUGIE: Ach naw, you're awright. I'll no need all that stuff. Daft to even bring it. Thanks and everything. By the way. For the projector. I didnae even know you needed a bloody projector! Built it up. I'll just tell yous it. Right. *(He gets out a wad of crumpled pieces of paper and starts to read. Formal. Rehearsed.)* Em. Eh. Right. "On Tuesday the 8th of August I received an email…"

LORENZO: Oh wait, wait…we should do a toast first.

ARLENE: Yeah! A toast to the young and a toast to the old. As one cage opens, another slams shut. Oh the humanity! Cheers! Ha ha ha!

LORENZO: That's a hellish toast.

DOUGIE: Em. "On Tuesday the 8th of August…"

ARLENE: *(Over the top of that.)* Fifty?! Oh my God that's just sunk in there. Fifty! Aaaah! Jesus Christ, how did that happen?

DOUGIE: Ach…I know what you mean…time just…

ARLENE: *(Over the top of him.)* Your bloody twenty first only seems like last year or something. God, we were married at *twenty one!* Jesus, your twenty first was bloody desperate. Remember? Back room of The Torrance Bar. We called it The Torrent. Trapped in The Torrent! *(To DOUGIE. A more troubling memory…)* And then your mum did that speech about me, mind?

DOUGIE: That was our engagement.

ARLENE: No, it was your twenty first. She really pulled out all the stops. Pointing at me. Cackling. Getting everyone to turn and look.

MOLLY: Why? What did she say?

ARLENE: *(Shrugs.)* It was my shaven head period. Doesn't matter. I got over it.

MOLLY: You looked so cool then.

ARLENE: His family didn't think so. In fact neither did mine.

DOUGIE: *(About the speech.)* Will I hingme? Keep going or…?

ARLENE: *(Continuing...)* And then of course she turned it round to her favourite subject. I was a...prepare yourself everyone...Catholic! Oh my God! The horror!

MOLLY: *(She's heard this before.)* I can't believe Nana gave a shit about all that stuff.

AARON: She doesn't anymore.

ARLENE: Aye but she did. By Christ she did! Even after we were married the Orange Walk would stop outside my mum and dad's front window. Honestly! Wee Jackie, at the side, all dressed up, self-righteous and saying nothing. *(Shaking it off.)* Ah to hell with all that. It's done. *(To DOUGIE, breezily.)* The Torrent burnt down didn't it?

DOUGIE: The Torrance? Naw.

ARLENE: Shame.

DOUGIE: I'm still in there. Thursdays. Quiz night. Big Rydo an that. Aaron comes in aw. Sure you do?

MOLLY: *(To AARON. Genuinely interested.)* Do you?

AARON: Well. Not anymore.

DOUGIE: Aye it's been two weeks or something you've no been there. Cannae bloody win without him. Music round an that.

MOLLY: *(To DOUGIE.)* I can come.

DOUGIE: No way.

MOLLY: Why not? I'm great in quizzes.

DOUGIE: Ach naw, it's...nah. Not a place for you, Molls.

MOLLY looks a little hurt by that, but DOUGIE doesn't clock it.

LORENZO: And how *is* your mum, Dougie? Keeping well?

DOUGIE: Eh. Aye. Uh huh.

LORENZO: She's quite a character, Jackie. Cracks me up.

DOUGIE: Aye.

LORENZO: Tremendous face. I keep saying I need to get a right good, tight-in headshot one of these days. Say to her will you?

DOUGIE: Uh huh.

ARLENE: Yeah, I wouldn't hold your breath for that one, babes.

LORENZO: I'm happy to go to her. No worries. My kit's in the car, ready to rock. Any time.

DOUGIE: She's made you some tablet Molls. For your exams and that.

LORENZO: Ach, that's very nice of her. Isn't it Molly?

MOLLY: Yeah. *(Deciding to brighten.)* Yeah, I love Nana's tablet. Pure sugar. Mmm.

DOUGIE: And listen. Thanks for…you know…having me here an' that.

LORENZO: Don't be daft.

ARLENE: We love having you here.

DOUGIE: I really hingme. Appreciate it an that. It's such a lovely house. Beautiful. I mean…totally lovely. Garden an aw. It's like a picture of something.

MOLLY: *(To DOUGIE, laughing.)* Dad!

DOUGIE: What?

MOLLY: You say that every time you come! It's so cute. It's like you've never been here before. You don't need to keep saying it's lovely.

DOUGIE: It is but. Beautiful…place. To live. Sorry. I didnae mean to…hingme.

MOLLY: And why do you always ring the bell? You've had a key for years. Just come in.

LORENZO: Me casa su casa.

MOLLY: It's cute but it's weird.

ARLENE: Molly, I've explained this. Your dad is a tourist in the big wide world. He thinks he's more visible than other folk or something. You should see him in a restaurant. He's a trembling wreck. *(She puts her empty glass on her head.)* Barkeep! There seems to be something wrong with my glass.

LORENZO takes the hint, and the glass.

LORENZO: Come anytime man. Honestly. During the day. We don't even need to be here. Just come in. Chill. We've got Sky Sports.

AARON: Oh. Talking of keys. I've still got a set of yours.

ARLENE: No, keep them. You never know, you might be back.

AARON: Nah, it's fine.

ARLENE: If your Uncle and your Gran are doing your nut in – need a wee breather – spare room's always there.

AARON: No. It's fine. Thanks anyway.

AARON separates the keys and gives them to ARLENE.

LORENZO: *(As he exits.)* Yeah, well the pair of you are welcome any time. You must be bouncing off the walls at your mum's place, Dougie.

LORENZO is off to the kitchen to get drinks.

DOUGIE: Ach, it's awright actually.

ARLENE: *(Troubled.)* Oh God. See when I think about you sleeping in that box room in your mum's ex-council…at fifty…I just feel so…tell me it's alright!

DOUGIE: It's fine aye.

ARLENE: And it's not forever, is it?

DOUGIE: Nah, it's…aye, it's awright.

ARLENE: And you don't even mind it, sure you don't?

DOUGIE: It's okay.

ARLENE: And I suppose it's nice for Aaron. His uncle and his granny – everyone under the same roof. *(A quick beat.)* Do yous talk?

AARON: No. We sit there in absolute silence. Day and night. It's like a monastery more than anything.

ARLENE: Seriously though, I mean…do yous chat about stuff?

DOUGIE: He's in his bloody room. This is the most I've heard him say since he came back. A fortnight a mumbles, no joke.

ARLENE: Okay.

Beat.

DOUGIE: Listen, should I keep going with the hingme? Presentation.

ARLENE: Wait for Lorenzo.

Pause.

DOUGIE: It is an amazing garden yous have got, man. Beautiful. I'd never seen a water feature in real life.

MOLLY and ARLENE laugh. AARON does too, a little bit.

DOUGIE has no idea why they're laughing. He smiles weakly.

Pause.

DOUGIE sighs. He looks at the picture of Saracen Bell and wonders… should I even do this? Saracen's eyes hold him.

ARLENE: And how's your mum, Aaron? Any progress?

AARON: I think so, thanks. Yeah, I think so.

ARLENE: Going through a good phase? Oh, that's good. Great.

AARON: Yeah…em…certainly…well, we're being optimistic.

ARLENE: Have they said when she'll be home?

AARON: There are discussions, I think. Wheels are turning. So. Anyway, we'll see. Aye.

ARLENE: Well, I'm sure it won't be long. Pair of you can get back into a flat of your own, start making plans for the future. Maybe you and your mum will get that big trip to Africa, eh? Remember that? Need some dough though, Aaron. Need a wee job to pay for that kind of thing. And you'll be delighted to get your sister back, won't you Dougie? *(No reply.)* Well. Happy days are on the way. Tell her I'm asking for her, will you? Next time you're up.

MOLLY: Is that horrible nurse still there? The one that wouldn't let you visit? Remember that? Didn't believe you were the son. Racist cow.

Beat.

DOUGIE: *(Deep breath and snapping out of it.)* Aye, she's showing signs of improvement. Everybody's very pleased.

LORENZO enters with drinks. He hands ARLENE a new G&T.

ARLENE: Ach, see…this is it in a nutshell.

LORENZO: What?

ARLENE: The first one had ice, a straw, a wedge of lime. Look at the state of that!

LORENZO: That's a gin and tonic. Exactly what you asked for.

ARLENE: No, this is a metaphor for married life, that's what this is, pal. When you first meet it's all sex and ice cubes. The ring goes on and boom – lime wedges long forgotten.

MOLLY: Aw gadz!

LORENZO: *(Grabbing ARLENE suggestively, playfully…)* I didn't know you were into lime wedging, ya dirty cow. Hey, I'm up for a bit of that. My safe word is "Brexit". Ha ha ha!

ARLENE: Ha ha ha! Gimmie some sugar you!

They kiss.

MOLLY: *(Screaming playfully.)* Oh my God! You guys! That is actually revolting! Stop it immediately or I swear I'll be sick in my own mouth. Disgusting, man!

They unhook. Laughing.

ARLENE: Ach loosen up, Molls. The Little Miss Frigid act won't play when you get to University you know. It'll be shag, shag, shag…lecture…shag, shag, shag…essay…shag, shag, shag…phone home to beg for money…Ha ha ha! See, maybe you shouldn't get a job after all, Aaron? Maybe you should go to Uni instead? Might be your one and only chance to lose your virginity! Ha ha ha! Naw, I'm only joking. You'll never lose your virginity. Ha ha ha!!!

AARON smiles weakly.

MOLLY: *(Laughing and covering her ears.)* No! You're horrible! I want a normal mum! Why can't I have a normal mum!

23

ARLENE: Don't pretend you're not gagging for it! Look at her! Counting the days till the shagfest begins!

MOLLY: Stop! Stop!

ARLENE and MOLLY are laughing.

LORENZO is handing DOUGIE a beer. LORENZO notices that DOUGIE's not taking this stuff too well. DOUGIE's not angry. He just looks like he might cry.

LORENZO: *(To ARLENE.)* Yeah c'mon Arlene. Behave. Inappropriate.

ARLENE: Oh dear, does Dougie disapprove? Sorry, Dougie! Sorry doll. But to be honest, Dougie comes from a family that doesn't touch – ever – so he's not the best when it comes to the lovey dovey stuff. Are you Doogs?

LORENZO: Doll, c'mon…

ARLENE: I'm not being funny. Never even shook your father's hand, did you? Never hugged his mother. Aaron knows. He grew up in that house too. Hey, I'm not slagging you, I was the same. They don't believe me! No emotion or expression in my family at *all…*'cept for when it all came bursting out like an exploding pressure cooker every fucking Saturday night. In my house affection was for the dog. Well I'm sorry, but that's not me anymore. *(Playfully dramatic.)* I'm free now! Free to embarrass my daughter! Free to fuck my husband!

LORENZO: Dougie's said nothing. It's me. Come on. It's a family party, clean it up.

ARLENE: You know what, Tinkie Winkie's right. It's getting far too racy in here. We need an insipid, PG-rated, family-friendly toast to calm us all down. Lorenzo, now is your time to shine.

LORENZO: I don't need to say anything if people don't want to…

ARLENE: Ah don't give us it! You only brought it up cos you're dying to do a speech. Probably practised it – look at the face! Come on, get it bloody over with.

LORENZO: Jeezo. Lovely build-up, eh? Alright. Everybody got a drink? Okay. *(His "host" voice.)* Hey. Look guys. All I want to say is…I happen to think we've got a lot to be thankful for here. And I don't just mean Molly's great results and getting into Uni and everything. And we're gonna miss you like hell, Toots. I can't even…I'm just not thinking about it! But listen, Sheffield's a great city. They gave us steel, The Human League and Pulp, so maybe it's only fair that we repay the debt by lending them you for a bit. And it's not that far really, so we'll be forever popping in for a cup of tea and a Pot Noodle – and yes, that is a threat! And I'm not talking about Dougie hitting the half century either. Which is, of course, also extremely awesome. No, I mean we should be thankful for the way we all get along. Families have changed, man. Back in the day we'd be enemies, right? But check us out! We should be proud of this! So here's to us, for all that we've achieved these last ten years or so. And here's to what we're all going to achieve in the future. The future!

They drink to "The Future". There's a smattering of applause from the others.

ARLENE: Jesus Christ. Telt ye. I feel carsick after that speech.

LORENZO: *(Smiling.)* Shut your face you. It was heartfelt!

MOLLY: Yeah. It was lovely, Lorenzo.

ARLENE: He's like a human version of one of those birthday cards with a watercolour rose on the front…"To my beloved Second Cousin on Bonfire Night. Here's to many more years of fellowship and care…"

LORENZO: Nah, you're a cynic that's your problem. A black-hearted cynic.

ARLENE: Only way to make it in this world baby, trust me.

MOLLY: I thought it was cool. Thanks Lorenzo.

LORENZO: Thank *you* Molly. I've always said you had a more refined taste than your scummy old mum.

ARLENE: Hey! Cheek! No, I'm only joking. Thanks Lorenzo, it was lovely. And I know I don't say this enough, but this family wouldn't survive if it wasn't for you. You did all the pick-ups and the drop-offs and the PTA and all that horrible shit. You raised Molly as much as I did. More maybe. You're a good man and you're going to Heaven. *(LORENZO and MOLLY laugh.)* Right. Douglas Bell. You're up.

DOUGIE: God. Follow that. Nervous now.

ARLENE: Well at least we know your speech won't give us diabetes.

ARLENE, MOLLY and LORENZO laugh again. AARON is watching DOUGIE intently – game time.

DOUGIE: It was a lovely speech, Lorenzo. Do you do a lot of speeches and that at your work?

LORENZO: Most of my stuff's online now, Dougie.

DOUGIE: Oh aye. So it is. God. You're very natural so you are.

ARLENE: Get on with it! God sake.

DOUGIE: Oh right. Okay. Right.

No getting out of it now. DOUGIE's trapped under glass. He clears his throat and pulls out the sheets of crumpled paper again. He starts to read.

As he does, ARLENE and LORENZO make eye contact and smile. They're not being nasty – DOUGIE's nervous, childlike reading just tickles them.

AARON sees them.

DOUGIE: *(Reading.)* "On Tuesday the 8th of August I received an email. I was very surprised. It was from a lawyer. I was very surprised." I was going to have the email up here but…it's not working so…em… *(Reading.)* "The lawyer was called Leonora Castle. She works for a company that has offices in Barbados, Atlanta, New York and London." There was a map but…know what I mean. I just couldnae get bloody PowerPoint tae…

ARLENE: PowerPoint is beyond you! We get it! Move on!

MOLLY: Mum!

ARLENE: What? It's taking longer than bloody *Lord of the Rings* this.

LORENZO: Keep going Dougie, it's fascinating. We're hooked. The lawyer emailed you and what did they say?

DOUGIE: Em. *(Reading.)* "Leonora Castle was based in the London branch. Her duties were to deal with cases in the UK. She said that there was a good chance she and her husband would be moving to Scotland because so many of her cases are now based"…em…cannae read that…
(Shows it to MOLLY.)

AARON: *(Under his breath.)* North of the border.

MOLLY: *(Reading.)* North of the border?

DOUGIE: Aye! It is. North of the border. I wrote it in aw! Cannae read my own bloody hingme! "Leonora explained that her firm represent The Journey Home Foundation. It was The Journey Home Foundation who discovered my case."

DOUGIE takes a drink and turns a page. He hasn't noticed, but everyone is listening now…

DOUGIE: *(Reading, with difficulty and occasionally gesturing behind him towards pictures that aren't there…)* "This is sugar cane. Sugar cane is any of several species of tall perennial true grasses of the genus Saccharum tribe. Sugar was the most important crop throughout the Caribbean. In the mid-17th Century sugar cane was brought into the British West Indies by the Dutch…

ARLENE: Right, woah woah woah. Take a breath there David Attenborough. I think you might've skipped a page.

DOUGIE: Eh?

ARLENE: What you on about?

DOUGIE: Sugar cane.

ARLENE: Let me rephrase the question. How come you're on about sugar cane?

DOUGIE: Cos that's how he made his money.

ARLENE: Who?

DOUGIE: Saracen Bell. *(He points at the photograph.)* That's William Bell. But they called him Saracen. He was a pure multi-millionaire. In his day. Like, I dunno, Bill Gates or something. There's books about him an everything. A Wikipedia page aw aboot him. It's pure amazing. That's where I'm getting this sugar stuff fae. Wikipedia. There's photos of his plantation in Jamaica an his palace in England. I had them aw here to show you but I couldnae get it…

ARLENE: *(Overlapping.)* Couldn't get it working, yeah I understand everything now. Just clear up a tiny detail… what's all this got to do with us?

DOUGIE: Well. That's the brilliant bit. I mean, it's pure *amazing* so it is. Absolutely…Arlene…honest tae God. It's amazing.

ARLENE makes an exasperated gesture. Tell us!

DOUGIE: *(Points at the photo. Delivering fantastic news…)* It's me. Me. I'm this guy's last living relative. It's obvious if you think about it. Dougie Bell. Saracen Bell. Bell.

LORENZO: You're his…what, you're related? To this guy?

DOUGIE: Aye.

MOLLY: Oh my God! Dad! That is so cool! We're related to a millionaire!

DOUGIE: That's what Leonora Castle was saying. In her email. Distant and that. Christ, I cannae even work out how tae say it…bloody fourth cousin once removed and aw that pish…but…it's a fact. We're aw that's left a' Saracen Bell.

There's a beat or two for that to settle a little.

MOLLY: Oh my God! It's like *Who Do You Think You Are?* or something!

DOUGIE: Do you think I look a wee bit like him? I think I look a wee bit like him. A wee bit.

ARLENE: And this guy was a millionaire?

DOUGIE: In modern money it's pure mental. Honest tae God.

ARLENE: And no one in your family thought to mention it?

DOUGIE: They didnae know! *(To AARON.)* Did they? It was pure ages ago.

ARLENE: So…is it about money then?

DOUGIE: What?

ARLENE: This.

DOUGIE: Aye. I explain it in my presentation. *(He holds up the paper for proof.)*

LORENZO: Holy shit! Wait. Is it…Dougie are you saying…you know…are you saying…?

DOUGIE: *(Interrupting. Delighted.)* It's *amazing*, sure it is? I've no been able to sleep since. I wanted to tell you as soon as I heard, but Aaron was like that, "Naw Uncle Dougie, yer birthday's coming up, going round to Lorenzo and Arlene's bit, save it for then, dae a hingme. Presentation." I wis like that, "awright".

AARON: Well I said it was an option. Seeing as we'd all be together and…

ARLENE: *(Coolly.)* So how much are we talking here?

DOUGIE: Well. Depends I suppose. But…close to twenty five grand.

LORENZO: Twenty five grand! Wow!

MOLLY: Oh my God! That could like…Dad. That could totally change…

AARON: No, no, it's not as much as that. It's five grand or something. I thought. Wasn't it?

DOUGIE: Naw. It's twenty five grand. I've checked. And that's just to start wi. If we can get more it'll be more. Know what I mean.

Pause.

ARLENE: *(Strained.)* Well. My goodness. Good for you Dougie.

MOLLY: This is *so* cool Dad! Oh my God!

DOUGIE: I know! I knew you'd think that. *(To AARON.)* See! Telt ye!

AARON: Yeah, it's just…I'm not sure everyone knows…are people clear what…?

DOUGIE: *(To everyone.)* I was nervous but…it makes sense dunt it?

AARON: I don't think people know what you're on about though, Uncle Dougie.

DOUGIE: It's aw in the speech. Will I bang on with the speech?

LORENZO: Woh, woh, woh! I need a beer. Anyone else want a drink?

ARLENE: Hell yeah.

DOUGIE nods and gives the thumbs up. LORENZO takes ARLENE's glass and hustles to the kitchen. DOUGIE's feeling really good.

LORENZO: *(Off.)* Keep going Dougie I can hear you.

DOUGIE: There's no much more to be honest. I emailed them and says aye and they're gonnie get back in touch wi aw the details an that. But I've got some stuff off a Wikipedia I can read. Aw the slavery stuff an that. It's no nice but.

ARLENE: Slavery stuff?

LORENZO's back with the drinks. He has his iPad under his arm. He hands out the booze and sits, opening the iPad.

LORENZO: What did you say his name was?

DOUGIE: William Bell. Type in Saracen Bell.

ARLENE: Why do you have stuff written down about slavery?

DOUGIE: Well…Cos that's what it's aw about int it?

MOLLY: Yeah! Shit. He'll've had slaves! We did it in Modern Studies. Sugar barons. Plantations. Oh my God. A slave master! We're actually related to a slave master! Oh my God.

LORENZO: *(The iPad.)* Here he is. The very fellow. "The Brutalities of Saracen Bell". Yeah there's loads look. University of Virginia. University of the West Indies…

MOLLY: Oh my God do you know what? It wasn't that long ago since when we all watched *12 Years a Slave*! And now we're all, like…connected to the story, kind of! Our family. Oh my *God!* That is freaky. That is so freaky!

ARLENE: *(To DOUGIE.)* What do mean "that's what it's all about"?

DOUGIE: Well…that's what it's all about.

ARLENE: *(Losing patience.)* It's not the fucking hokey-cokey, Dougie. Explain it. *Why* is that what it's all about? How is this "all about" slavery?

LORENZO: *(Still on the iPad.)* Oooooh. Guess who else is related to a slave owner? Benedict Cumberbatch.

MOLLY: No way! He was *in 12 Years a Slave*! Oh my God I am freaking out!

LORENZO: George Orwell too. David Cameron. What a surprise. Bloody knew it. Hang your head Cameron.

DOUGIE: They'll be part of The Journey Home Foundation. Bet you any money. It's what you do, she says. Even if you cannae pay now you sign up to the pledge. Know what I mean.

ARLENE: No. We don't know what you mean. What do you mean? Aaron. Tell me.

AARON: Reparation.

DOUGIE: I says that. Reparation.

ARLENE: Reparation?

DOUGIE: Aye. That's what I said. It means like…

ARLENE: I know what it means.

MOLLY: What does it mean?

ARLENE: *(Getting it.)* So the twenty five grand is for…?

DOUGIE: Aye. For reparation. Like I says, if I can find more than twenty five grand I'll give them more than twenty five grand, but they seem to reckon twenty five is as good a starting point as anything.

AARON: It can be less though. It can be anything really.

MOLLY: I don't know what it means. What does reparation mean?

ARLENE: It's payment. It's like a…

DOUGIE: It makes sense if you think about it, sure it does? You cannae say it doesnae. *(To LORENZO.)* Get the website up a minute, Lorenzo. It's good. There's different sections.

MOLLY: I don't get it.

AARON: The Journey Home Foundation are asking your dad…to give *them*…money. Okay? Then they'll distribute that money to the families of the people that Saracen Bell had em…enslaved. The money goes to the people who need it most. In the here and now. Obviously. So it's…you know. It's good.

DOUGIE: Everyone does it. It's called The Journey Home Foundation.

MOLLY: You pay them? For what he did? But…are they *making* you pay?

DOUGIE: Naw. They're no *making* me, they're asking me. But like, who's *no* gonnie pay?

ARLENE: Oh I dunno. Maybe someone who works part time in a supermarket, sleeps in the box room of their mother's ex-council house and doesn't have a penny to his name?

LORENZO: *(Still eyes down at the iPad.)* "The Journey Home Foundation." Yeah. Pretty basic site…

AARON: Well the format's quite basic but the roots are sound.

DOUGIE: *(Over that.)* Click on hingme. "Atrocities".

ARLENE: No. Go to "About".

He does. ARLENE takes the iPad from LORENZO…

LORENZO: Have you had any face time with anyone, Dougie?

DOUGIE: *(A weight is off his shoulders and the words are flowing out now…)* Naw, but see when the email came in I was like that…at last. At *last*, man! It was like I was kinda, waiting on it or something. Cos see for like…donkeys, I've been like that… "what's the point in life man?".

MOLLY: Oh, charming!

DOUGIE: No! I don't mean…aye, you're my total reason for staying alive Molls, don't get me wrong. *(A glance to AARON.)* Aaron in aw. But, know what I mean, yous are done now. Grown up and that. And it's just me and I just…I'm fifty, right. If I don't do something now I never will. Know what I mean? Something a wee bit…bigger. Something that counts.

LORENZO: Have you got the emails there on your phone?

DOUGIE: Naw. I'm no explaining it very well. Jist…like… well…it's awright at mum's. But see some nights, I'm just lying on my bed like that… "How did this happen? This is where I am, but how did this actually *happen*? Who's to blame for this?"

AARON: Yeah, I don't think The Journey Home Foundation is about "blame" so much as…

DOUGIE: *(Cont.)* And then there was this programme on, right…about dictators, an it got me pure thinking. I love dictators an aw that so I do. Well, see when Napoleon was a prisoner on hingme…that island.

LORENZO: St Helena. I've been there.

DOUGIE: *(Cont.)* …well there were aw these giant tortoises, like, in his garden. Pets. And you know what…they're still there! Well, one of them is anyroads. They don't know for sure, you cannae tell their ages bang on, but it's a fair bet that this exact same tortoise was there when Napoleon was there.

LORENZO: Yeah, it's a crazy place, man. I did some filming on it when I was with Endemol. Impossible to get to. We had to charter a boat and it was touch and go let me tell you. Perfect Storm stuff. But beautiful…like, locked in time. I'll tell you where else is amazing for that…the Faroe Islands.

MOLLY: *(To DOUGIE.)* Dad…

DOUGIE: I'm no explaining it very well but...like...Napoleon was important. Sure he was? Mair important than me anyways. An at the end of the day, when they're chalking up aw the human beings that have achieved shit...good or bad...his name is on that list. Int it? He must've thought he was immortal or something. But he's fucking *nothing* compared to that tortoise. Know what I mean? Napoleon's gone. But that tortoise is still there. An aw this shit that we're on about – *(the photo)* aw this – it happened in that tortoise's lifetime.

MOLLY: Dad...?

DOUGIE: Christ. I'm talking absolute pish, man! Tortoises?! It's this bloody chocolate beer! Can I get one of my Tennent's, Lorenzo? Please. Would that be okay?

LORENZO: You're kidding me, man? Try a Valentino IPA instead.

DOUGIE: Ach, naw, you're awright.

LORENZO: They're perfumed.

DOUGIE: Aye, naw, you're awright.

LORENZO: No, try one. Honestly I've loads. You know that band Valentino Drag? It's them that make it. It's Scottish and there's none of that bloody...

DOUGIE: *(Shouting.)* Just give me a fucking can of Tennent's Lager please!

ARLENE: *(Matching his pitch.)* Don't you fucking speak to him like that!

DOUGIE: *(Immediately.)* I'm so sorry. I...sorry, Lorenzo. Sorry. I'm just...nervous from all the...

LORENZO: *(Genuinely.)* Oh hey, hey, hey it's cool! Totally cool. Absolutely. No worries. One Tennent's coming right up. Absolutely. Molls? *(MOLLY shakes her head.)* Aaron? *(AARON lifts the bottle from earlier, shaking his head, he's hardly touched it. To ARLENE.)* Babe? Refresh?

ARLENE: *(To LORENZO.)* Aye.

LORENZO exits to the kitchen...

MOLLY: Dad, are you in trouble?

No answer. DOUGIE is composing himself.

ARLENE: *(To DOUGIE.)* Dougie, this website is nothing.

ARLENE has a thought and gives AARON a quick, searching look. He holds her eye for a beat until she's distracted by DOUGIE...

DOUGIE: *(Over the top of them.)* Naw, look...I'm sorry I kinda got like...I'm just getting aw...it's a big thing this. For me. And aw I know is...and this is what I was trying to say with the bloody tortoises...we're alive, right? Me, you...bloody Napoleon...for *(snaps his fingers)* that! Right? Nothing. In the scheme of things...blink and it's away. And what do we do?

ARLENE: Right, stop. Okay? You're making a fool of yourself. We need to talk about this *(the iPad)*.

DOUGIE: But I'm never gonnie be Napoleon. Am I? I know that. But shouldn't I try an do something a wee bit... fucking...bigger? If I get the chance. Bigger than what I am now I mean? I want to do something *good!*

ARLENE: Stop swearing in front of Molly! Lower your voice and sit down. Now. Sit down!

He does. LORENZO is back with the drinks...

ARLENE: Cheers. *(To DOUGIE.)* Right...look...I know you. You'll've built this all up in your head and not given a single thought to the realities of the matter...

DOUGIE: Ach...

ARLENE: You're picturing crowds of grateful fans in Jamaica mobbing you in the street – weeping with joy like you're Abraham Lincoln or Martin Luther King or something. And there's you, making it rain with fivers...

That hits the bullseye...

ARLENE: *(Cont.)* But see this site...it's nothing. You need to take a deep breath here.

DOUGIE: How do I?

ARLENE: Well, first off you need to find out if it's even real.

DOUGIE: Aye it's real.

ARLENE: You don't know that for sure, Dougie.

DOUGIE: *(Getting angry.)* Click on "Atrocities"! That'll tell you what's real. Know what I mean. God sake Arlene.

LORENZO: *(At the iPad again.)* Saracen Bell *is* everywhere, doll. Can't fake that. Books, paintings…

ARLENE: I'm not saying…

DOUGIE: *(Getting up, getting big…)* Go to "Atrocities"! Go to "Atrocities"! Cos see when they left Africa, right, they had to walk through this pure massive gate before they got on the boat. It was called The Door Of No Return. And they *knew* that was what it was called. Imagine going through that door…with your kid holding your hand. Gripping your hand. The kids hoping the mums and the dads are gonna make everything okay again. And the mums and the dads knowing exactly what was coming next. Naw. They cannae stop it. And it will never be okay again. There is no return. An see when those kids got sick, on the boat, going over…and they *did* get sick – aw the time, right – cos they were aw chained thegither and squeezed into tiny wee shelves below deck for ten weeks or something, on the high seas…well, see when the kids got sick, stopped eating, started wasting away…they'd drag them up on deck and they'd whip them. Cos they were losing value, right? So they'd whip them. As an example to the others. Whipping fucking toddlers…two years old…three years old…whipping them…sometimes to death. And if the sick wee kids died…and jist…jist…picture that a minute: a three year old kid killed by a whip! Must've been like… pulp, bone, gore, just like, fucking unrecognisable wee bodies…well, if they died, then they'd make the mum take the corpse and chuck it over the side. And they'd make the mum *watch* as the wee thing dropped into the fucking sea. And if the mum refused to watch, or turned her head away, or cried, then the mum got whipped. And for that they made the *fathers* watch. Everybody wanting to scream. But they couldnae scream. And they wouldnae stop. Cos it never stopped. Nothing can stop this. Well…anyway…see that shit…that was just it *starting*. That was the *start* of what happened to they folk. No that long ago. Go to "Atrocities", Arlene. Go to "Atrocities". Because, let me tell you: it's fucking real.

There's a big pause.

MOLLY: Oh my God.

MOLLY is crying a wee bit. ARLENE comforts her, giving DOUGIE a cold look as she does…

DOUGIE: *(Controlling himself now.)* And the thing is…right… turns out…it was us. It was us that done it to them. Us.

Another pause.

LORENZO: Yeah. I mean…totally. Yeah, we like to blame England for the Empire and…em…but Glasgow…you know. Built on tobacco…sugar… *(Indicating the house they're in)* all these mansions, man…where do you think they came from?

DOUGIE: It was us. Sure it was Lorenzo? It was us.

LORENZO: It's not called Jamaica Street cos we dig reggae.

DOUGIE: Know what I mean! Aye. It was totally us. *(Pointing at Saracen Bell.)* And it was *actually* us. Like…It's in my blood! *Our* blood, Molly. It's horrible, right, but me and you are in this, like it or no, we're in it. Aaron in aw. In his own way. This is our mess. Too right this is a real thing. This is a fucking real thing.

ARLENE: Of *course* slavery is a real thing. I'm not saying it isnae. I'm saying this organisation, this "foundation"…

DOUGIE: I got an email from them, Arlene!

ARLENE: *(Taking a breath. Trying to steer this back a little.)* Alright. Okay. Dougie. I've met your family. Aunts, uncles, cousins you name it. I've met them all. And there's no money there.

DOUGIE: Aye, but…

ARLENE: Aaron. Back me up. Factory workers, dinner ladies, electricians, shop girls…Uncle Whatshisname – the great star of the brood – he was a policeman. Okay, he was promoted and in the paper every now and then, but he was a policeman. Everyone else was a bloody farmer.

LORENZO: Yeah but doll…it only takes a generation for things to…

DOUGIE: Aye exactly! It was the generations…It was like years and years and years…

ARLENE: But that's what I'm saying…there's no trace of money anywhere on your family tree. *(Pointing at Saracen.)* Money like that – great big, fuck-off, heaving oceans of horrible money – that leaves its mark man. You can still see it, generations later, you can see it on people's skin – battered in. Benedict Cumberbatch…David Cameron… aye, okay I can believe that. I buy it. *Downton Abbey* stuff. Okay. But see you…you're below stairs. All of your family…below stairs. And that's on your skin too.

DOUGIE: This is a real thing.

There's a pause.

ARLENE was trying not to do this, but here it comes…

ARLENE: Well. There was a time when you thought selling Juice Pills was a real thing. Didn't you? And look what happened to that.

DOUGIE probably saw that coming, but it still hits him hard. He's still very ashamed about that fiasco…

DOUGIE: *(Quietly.)* Fuck sake.

LORENZO: Yeah, c'mon doll that's water under the bridge. We all decided that we wouldn't…

ARLENE: I'm not doing anything. I'm just saying. We've been here before, haven't we?

DOUGIE: This is a totally different thing.

ARLENE: Is it?

DOUGIE: I paid him back. Sure I did, Lorenzo? I paid you back?

LORENZO: Absolutely. Don't mention it, Dougie. Honestly.

ARLENE: Didn't pay it *all* back.

LORENZO: Look. C'mon. It's fine. We agreed a scheme. He paid back what he could. Everybody's cool.

DOUGIE: I paid back what I could.

LORENZO: And I was totally utterly happy with that. We all were. So it's cool. It was ages ago anyway. We're all pals here. Come on. Hey, what happened to the bloody party, man?

DOUGIE: And anyway, how is that the same as this?

ARLENE: We don't know if it is. Yet.

DOUGIE: I'm telling you. It's no the same.

ARLENE: Something's the same. You're standing in our living room asking for money to fund a plan that sounds super dodgy from the get-go. That rings a bell or two.

DOUGIE: Naebody knew that the juice thing was…and they worked! They did work. They pills. And I paid yous back. Tried to anyway. They were a real thing that just didnae kinda…

ARLENE: Aye well, for all we know you're on some kind of database somewhere…

LORENZO: Doll, come on…

ARLENE: *(Cont.)* Some list of the nation's suckers…

MOLLY: Mum this is different…

ARLENE: *(Cont.)* All the gullibles lumped thegither ready to be milked and this is just the latest in a long line of scams.

LORENZO: Right, Arlene come on. We're talking about bloody slavery here.

ARLENE: No we're not, Lorenzo! Try to keep up.

LORENZO: It's just that…if this *is* true…then as a family…I think we probably have some degree of…well…

ARLENE: What? Responsibility? No. We don't. Cos if this is legit – which it isn't – but if it is…it wasn't us that did it!

It was someone else…generations ago. Are we meant to be paying the families of folk our granddads killed in the Second World War? This is history. And anyway, it's *not* our family. *(About DOUGIE.)* It's *his* family. So if he wants to give his money to this scam then by all means let him pile in. But he's not getting anything from us. *(To DOUGIE.)* Okay? Which might be a wee bit of a problem for you, eh Dougie? Cos you don't actually have any money of your own. Do you? No. So. Let's just forget your wee *Dragons' Den* pitch here, pack up the presentation and have a drink.

DOUGIE: I'm no asking you for money.

ARLENE: *(Sarcastically.)* I believe you.

DOUGIE: I'm no.

A silence as ARLENE counts to ten. Then…

ARLENE: Finished. Okay? I'm smiling. Clean sheet. I'm going to put some food in the oven and open a bottle of fizz – which I intend to tank. I'm smiling. See? Let's finish on a smile shall we?

DOUGIE: I have the money.

ARLENE: *(Heading for the kitchen.)* I doubt it, but good for you.

DOUGIE: Molly's account. Know what I mean.

ARLENE stops and turns.

There's nearly twenty five grand in it now. So. That's absolutely ideal. Sure it is? You need to sign it too but. The form. Withdrawal. I've got it with me. *(He holds up a bank form.)* So. That's how come I'm telling ye. Doesnae have to be the night though.

ARLENE is stunned. She might even laugh at the audacity of it all. DOUGIE is under no illusions as to the task ahead. He can't quite meet her eye.

ARLENE moves back towards him…she is very close to explosion…

ARLENE: You are…oh…I…you have *got* to be joking? Right? Tell me. Tell me this is all some kind of funny…

DOUGIE: Naw. It's…It's the money I got when dad died. Sure it is? That's just a fact. He got it from his pay-out and he left it to me. I'd forgotten it was there, truth be told, but yous were on about it the other night and I thought, no, here, wait a minute. So it's…I'm no asking for *your* money. Just…you know…just my money.

ARLENE: The…so…sorry…explain this…you're saying that's *your* money now are you? Molly's account. That's your money?

DOUGIE: It *is* my money.

ARLENE: The money that's going to pay for Molly's first year at University? Her University money? The only fucking good thing you have *ever* contributed to in her entire life? That's *your* money now is it? And you want to take it *back*?!

DOUGIE: She…she doesnae need it. I don't think.

ARLENE: She doesn't *need* it? She goes to University in one month! Of course she fucking needs it!

DOUGIE: Ach, you know what I mean.

ARLENE: Tell her then.

MOLLY: Mum I think we should talk about this…

ARLENE: Tell her you're taking away her University fund! Go on! Tell her!

DOUGIE: You don't need that money. Christ man, look at where you live!

ARLENE slaps DOUGIE…once…twice…three times.

LORENZO and MOLLY jump up and pull her away – shouting and appealing for calm as they do. AARON goes to DOUGIE but DOUGIE pushes him away roughly.

DOUGIE didn't even really protect himself. He comes out of the scuffle a little changed: a half-hidden, wry wee grin on his lips as he checks for blood. The hint of a swagger. He's assured, somehow, by her violence…

DOUGIE: Spit of yer oldboy eh, Arlene? In wi the fists. Exact same. Always wur.

ARLENE: The one good thing you've done for her! The *only* good thing. And you want to take it away? No. Never. I won't let you. No way!

DOUGIE: Aye but it's mine.

ARLENE: Aye but it's no! It's ours. Naw. It's *hers*. We promised her. You'll *never* get it. Never. So that's that.

AARON: Right I think if we just…I think what Uncle Dougie is trying to…see, I suppose, it's just, legally speaking…

ARLENE: *(Fury.)* Honestly? Honestly?!

LORENZO: Babe, come on…

ARLENE: *(LORENZO.)* Are you hearing this? Lawyers?!

DOUGIE: Don't get at Aaron, he's in the right.

ARLENE: *(To DOUGIE.)* What are you saying to me ya fucking little failure?!

AARON: I'm not saying lawyers. I'm just saying that legally… em…well, you know, legally…

ARLENE: Legally what? Speak! The legal expert! Last month the police are bringing him back drunk, today he's a lawyer!

LORENZO: Look, shoosh, shoosh…There's no need for lawyers. There's no need for violence. There's no need for anything. Why don't we all just…

ARLENE: Oh shut up Lorenzo! That's not bloody violence. Don't call that violence. You don't know what you're talking about. Fuck sake.

DOUGIE: *(Still to ARLENE.)* Aye and by the way, see if you want a taste of real violence, click on "Atrocities".

MOLLY: I don't mind. I…I…I honestly mum, I don't mind. Dad should have that money. If he wants it.

ARLENE: No. Don't you worry Molly doll this is a veto. It's a fucking guillotine. *(Smacks her hands like a blade coming down.)* No! No! No! Never.

MOLLY: I can get a job or…like, I dunno…take a year out…?

ARLENE: No. It's too late. This is your chance.

MOLLY: It's important to Dad and if it was his money in the first place…

ARLENE: *(To DOUGIE.)* Hear that?

DOUGIE: What?

ARLENE: Can you hear your only daughter speaking?

DOUGIE: Aye. Can *you*? She's being reasonable. Unlike some.

ARLENE: God almighty. It's…you see the surface and that's all. You see the water ripple but you have no idea what's going on in the depths below. You don't even know there *are* depths below!

MOLLY: I want Dad to be happy that's all.

ARLENE: She's asking you to let her keep that money.

MOLLY: I'm not.

DOUGIE: She's not. She's on my side. She's always been on my side. *(To MOLLY.)* We're the same sure we are, Molls? Peas in a pod.

ARLENE: No. I let you say that every bloody birthday and Christmas and God knows what, but naw. I'm not having it tonight. You gave her your bad teeth and that money. End of. The list of what separates you, however, is vast. And I'd say, as proven once again by your little "presentation" this evening, that number one on that list is the fact that she is clever…and you, son…are fucking thick.

There are reactions. But no one speaks for a bit…

ARLENE: Oh dear. The great unsaid. We must never say that someone is more intelligent than someone else must we? Even when it's staring you in the face. Look in her eyes and tell me she's not brighter than you in every conceivable way.

DOUGIE: I know that. I'm no arguing that.

ARLENE: We're all meant to be the same these days eh? All equal. But it's a crock. You're thick, she's clever.

43

DOUGIE: I know! I know that! I've known that since she was a tiny baby. And I'll tell you something else, that's fine with me man! That's what I want.

ARLENE: Then how can you stand in the way of her getting a bloody education?

DOUGIE: I'm not. One hing's got nothing to dae with the other.

ARLENE: You're scared you'll lose all sight of her as she flies away, like you lost sight of me. So you're going to hold her down, clip her wings.

DOUGIE: No! I want her to go to Uni. I love her and she loves me.

ARLENE: Sure about that? Can someone really love a person who isn't as clever as they are? Don't think so. They can pretend, but it's not love, it's something else.

DOUGIE: Oh, what, are you saying she doesnae love me now? My daughter doesnae love me cos I'm thick?

MOLLY: Mum! Don't say…I do so love Dad. I do! Oh my God. Don't say…take it back!

ARLENE: Okay, okay, okay. I take it back. Maybe it's just me that cannae love him.

That comment hangs in the air for a big beat or two…

DOUGIE: It isnae even about you, Molly. Honest. This is about doing something good. This is about making up for all the…fucking… *(viciously jabbing a finger at Saracen Bell and shouting)*…BAD!

ARLENE shakes her head. Her heart's still thumping, but when she speaks she seems calm and reasonable. As far as she's concerned this is done now.

ARLENE: I'm going to get the food going. It's just nibbles. Stuff to pick at. You can stay. But that… *(the projection of Saracen Bell)*…that goes. And this subject is closed. We're civilised. Okay, Dougie? There's nothing you can do about this, so don't even try. It's done.

ARLENE exits to the kitchen.

*DOUGIE throws his speech to the ground in anger. He closes his eyes…
he's taking deep breaths…trying to get some control of this…trying to
find his next move and stave off the defeat and all that comes with
it…he starts to pace like an animal in a cage…*

LORENZO: *(To DOUGIE, about ARLENE.)* You two. Really push
each other's buttons eh? Passionate folk the pair of you. I
really…like, you know, Dougie….the passion you feel for
this cause it's…quite inspiring. It really is. So, listen man,
here's what I'm going to do. If you can verify this…just…
you know…a little bit of research…if you can show me that
this is all totally kosher, because it sounds…well, anyway,
I would seriously consider giving you a wee bit of money
myself. And not as a loan. A gift. And that's no lie.

DOUGIE: I'm no asking for your money.

LORENZO: Oh I know. I know that, yeah. Sure. Okay. Well.

DOUGIE: I'm asking for *my* money.

LORENZO: Well…

DOUGIE: And an apology.

AARON pricks up his ears – this is new.

LORENZO laughs. DOUGIE rounds on him.

DOUGIE: What's funny about that?

LORENZO: Nothing. It's just that…

DOUGIE: I want an apology. From her.

LORENZO: Yeah. No, sorry man, I didn't mean to laugh.
I thought you were taking the piss.

DOUGIE: Why would you think that? She's never said sorry.
Not once. I'm owed that. Right? At the very least someone
needs to say fucking sorry.

LORENZO: Yeah but, you know…do you mean for…?

DOUGIE: For this! For the state we're in. A bloody apology is
the very *least* I should get, man.

LORENZO: Yeah. Look mate. I think, em…right, I have this
lawyer pal…Ben. You met him at our Eurovision party,

remember? Well anyway, Ben won't take a case if there's been an apology. If you've already said sorry – even in the immediate aftermath of a car crash or something – nup. Bye bye. Turns you away. You've already lost.

DOUGIE: What's that got to do wi anything?

AARON: And I don't think it's very fair that some people can talk about lawyers but some people can't.

LORENZO: What's that pal?

AARON: I'm just saying…you know. I talk about lawyers and Arlene totally…she physically assaulted Uncle Dougie there. We all saw it. But you can talk about lawyers and it's fine. I don't think that's fair.

LORENZO: No, I'm saying…

AARON: It's like there's one rule for one, another for another.

LORENZO: No, I'm just saying, like, an apology can be considered a…em…a…eh. Ach. I dunno. *(Beat.)* I can ask her. I'll ask her. *(An unconvincing change of tone.)* Hey! I'm for getting gassed. Who's with me? Molly? You got a drink? Aaron! Come on man. Want another one?

AARON: No thank you. I don't really like it.

LORENZO: Something else then?

AARON: No thank you.

LORENZO: Please?

AARON: No thank you.

A beat. Then…

LORENZO goes to the laptop and quickly does what he has to do to get rid of the projection…

LORENZO: I'll check on her. See what she says. But em… don't…and I'll get the beers in too, don't panic! Ha!

He goes off after ARLENE. DOUGIE's looking at the wall where Saracen used to be.

AARON comes over to the laptop, hits a few keys and Saracen Bell's picture returns.

AARON: *(To DOUGIE.)* You didn't say that thing about it having to sting.

DOUGIE: Eh?

AARON: About how you need to feel the sting for it to mean something. I think the word "sting" is good.

MOLLY: I'll take a year out.

DOUGIE: Naw…

MOLLY: I'll take a year out.

DOUGIE: Nah, look…

MOLLY: I don't mind. Kara's doing it.

DOUGIE: You'll get to University, doll. And you're gonnie be fine no matter what. Everything coming your way is gonnie be good – no dark corners. Know what I mean? You're going to Uni and you're getting your nice, pure life and I'll…bloody…*destroy* anyone that stands in the way a that. Don't care who it is. I swear to God.

MOLLY: If you don't want me to have that money though…

DOUGIE: *(Frustrated.)* No! You think I don't want *you* to have it, but it's no that. It's nothing to do wi you. I…ach, I dunno. I cannae explain it.

A pause. Then…

AARON: I think…I think it's just that your dad has to be the one that hurts, Molly. *(To DOUGIE.)* Sure you do?

DOUGIE: Aye.

AARON: It has to be him that stings. His pain. His money. It has to hurt *him*. Cos it's his responsibility. It's his fault. *(Again to DOUGIE. With a tiny bit of edge.)* Sure it is?

DOUGIE: Aye. It has to be my money. No their money. It's me making the sacrifice, no them.

AARON: *(To MOLLY.)* And I know you're on side with this, I really do, cos it fits in with everything you say. Your ideals. All our discussions. I knew nothing about politics and all that shit until you turned me on to it, Mols. I've never forgotten that conversation we had, right there, last Christmas Day, and it was suddenly like we were meeting for the first time, even though I've known you all my life! I was like that, "who *is* this person?". "Why have I been sitting in my room doodling when all this was going on in the big wide world?!". Only, see this, it isn't "the big wide world" this is right here, right now! It's not an online petition or a discussion group or a march in George Square. Molly, this is something we can actually do. This will make a difference.

DOUGIE: Cos it was us.

AARON: Something happened that was cruel and unfair and ruined lives and we can make up for it. There are stories without ends and folk without families and we can make up for it.

DOUGIE: You'll still go to Uni doll.

AARON: Of course you will! *(About ARLENE and LORENZO.)* They're loaded. It's a drop in the ocean for them. Convince your mum to sign that form and off you go – clean.

DOUGIE: That's right.

MOLLY: What you talking about, "clean"? How does that even…?

AARON: Well, I don't know, it'll be like a border or something. A firewall. For all of us. Absolved. Clean. However you want to say it. I think you know what I mean.

DOUGIE: I know what you mean. We're doing something good and making up for the bad.

There's a pause. MOLLY can see that AARON's words have affected DOUGIE. There's something about AARON's manner – and his role here – that makes her uneasy…

AARON: Cos think about it…you are either the *enemy* of Saracen Bell – determined that no trace of him shall survive, manifest in your bloodstream or in your morality – or you are endorsing him. "Crazy Old Uncle Saracen. My, he was a one. Mind you, we're all a bit like that in my family."

MOLLY: No. Wait a minute, it doesn't work like that.

AARON: His blood is in your veins.

MOLLY: It's in your veins too. Genetics doesn't mean that everyone's exactly the same all the way down the line.

AARON: Yeah, I got an A in Biology Molly, thanks very much.

MOLLY: Well you should know then. Things change.

AARON: In Biology. Not in History.

MOLLY: *(Harder.)* I got an A in History.

AARON: And was one of the questions: "Are you for or against slavery?"

MOLLY: Oh come on! It's more complex than that.

AARON: *(Getting angry.)* Is it? Honestly? Look me in the face and tell me there are grey areas to this.

DOUGIE: I'm against slavery. So I am. Totally. Totally against it. I think reparation is…know what I mean?

AARON: *(Over the top of him, becoming animated.)* And what would you do if it turned out that one or more of us *was* like him? Already? Eh? What if it turned out that people had… *(Stops himself.)*

MOLLY: What?

DOUGIE: Talk your mum, Molls. She'll listen to you.

AARON: *(To MOLLY. Under control, just…)* You told me once that if a system is corrupt then the only way forward is to smash it up and start again. So smash it up.

MOLLY: Smash what up? What are you…?

AARON: I don't see what the problem is here? You don't get hurt. The Golden Girl gets what she wants, as always, and the world keeps turning. Only for once you could actually be helping someone instead of just fucking talking about it!

MOLLY: Why are you shouting at me? Why am I the enemy here?

DOUGIE: You're not the enemy, doll. *(Saracen.)* He is.

AARON: And no one's shouting. Okay. Right. Another way to look at this is…em…ask yourself, what would be the *right* thing to do? Not politically or economically or what's best for family dynamics or any of that shit…what's the *right* thing to do as a *human being*? It might feel tough at first, but that's just how justice has to work sometimes.

MOLLY: Oh, so it's justice now? I see. And are you my judge Aaron?

AARON: No. I'm the guy standing up for you!

MOLLY: How is this you standing up for me? And anyway it's been me standing up for *you*! I've been helping *you*! All through school, people picking on you, calling you names, calling you weird, it's me that steps in! It was me that convinced Mum and Lorenzo to let you move in here. Which was working, right? Don't deny it, you were back to your old self and then bang! The door slams and you're gone. And now this. This is…there's something wrong with this, man. It's not the money. It's what it's gonna…I think it might…this might not be fixable.

Beat.

AARON: Some things aren't fixable. See the stuff that happened here…this…it's more than a crime. Much, much more than a crime. It's a moral abomination. It's a century worth of holocaust. On your command. You. You're the ones that did it. And what have you paid? Absolutely nothing. You. Your family. Your city. Your country. This bloody country – that we can't stop talking about and praising and defining and defending and having fucking referendums about – it committed a holocaust. And got away with it. We *have* to smash it up. Smash it up and get the hell out.

MOLLY: I don't know what you're…I haven't done anything wrong!

DOUGIE: Aye, but, see Molls…think about it. What did they give up? What would the world be like now if this shit never happened? Know what I mean?

AARON: People could've had different lives…mothers and fathers…entirely different lives…if not for the actions of someone in our family years ago. Put it that way.

DOUGIE: So…you know…you've had an amazing life… beautiful house and wonderful…garden…Sky Sports… bloody…great, brilliant people everywhere…you've never had to…kinda…deal with aw the…and I'm happy about that don't get me wrong…but see most folk? They live a much harder life than you. They have to fight and work and it's windy and cold.

MOLLY: Dad, I work.

DOUGIE: I know you do and that's fine, but it's no graft is it?

MOLLY: How do you know?

DOUGIE: Aye, I'm no saying…it's just like…folk like Aaron… it's harder for him than it is for you.

MOLLY: I work harder than he does. He doesn't work. He's never had a job. I don't even think he's even *applied* for a job. Never tried for college or university even though he could.

AARON: Oh could I? Thanks very much Molly.

DOUGIE: Right…don't get at Aaron. It's different for him. Tougher than it is for you.

MOLLY: Yeah, only cos he makes it tough. It's a choice.

AARON: Oh, this is a choice is it? I chose this?! Wow.

MOLLY: Getting off your nut all the time was a choice…not phoning that number Lorenzo gave you at the website place was a choice…hanging about with dad and his pals all day is a choice.

DOUGIE: Right, shoosh Molly. Come on. Aaron's life is tougher than yours, it just is.

MOLLY: Again…how do *you* know? You don't have a clue what my life is like. You're not here.

DOUGIE: *(The house.)* I can see what it's like.

MOLLY: Not everything is visible to the naked eye, Dad! What's it like being me? Can you tell by looking? Can I drop out and watch TV all day? Can I give work and education a "by" please? Can I choose?! Anything! Anything to do with my own life. Can I make a *choice*? Just once! Can I?!

DOUGIE: All I'm saying is sometimes things are better if you've earned them. Know what I mean?

MOLLY: Right. So you *do* want to take the money from me?

DOUGIE: No…

MOLLY: Yes you do. That's what you're saying. You want to take something away from me. So that I can feel the "sting" of your terrible life? Am I getting that line right, Aaron?

DOUGIE: *Their* life! No mine. It's *their* life I'm talking about. The slaves. You've had everything given – they had it all taken away.

MOLLY: *(Really angry now.)* I said you could have the money! Have the money!

DOUGIE: I'm just…it's a father's job to make sure the children know what the world is really like. Know what I mean. Prepare the children. Some things that you think are forever can be just…taken away.

MOLLY: Like what?

DOUGIE: Well, I dunno. Anything. Everything. Just, like, know what I mean…you've had all this…wonderful stuff… given to you. You expect it. Everywhere you go. But see sometimes, you have to, you know…

MOLLY: What? Earn it? So I have to earn your love? Or you'll take it away? Is that what you're saying?

DOUGIE: Eh? No. No!

MOLLY: Am I being taught or am I being punished here Dad, cos let's face it, you haven't done much of either in my life so I'm a bit confused. And I'm sorry, but what's so wrong with expecting a father's love?

AARON: Because not everyone gets it. Where's mine, eh? On the run from the first sight of a dirty nappy, right? And I don't even get to cling to the *idea* of a... *(suddenly stops himself and snaps at MOLLY.)* You know something I can't fucking believe you're arguing against this! It's...I tell you man, I did not plan for that.

MOLLY: What did you plan for?

LORENZO enters. He has drinks and food on a tray.

LORENZO: Right, no judgement please, and don't say anything, but Arlene's in the garden chain smoking. First time in, what, three years or something? I'm not asking where she got the fags from cos that would be... but anyway. Just nobody say anything cos she'll feel shite enough without us all chiming in, believe me. *(He sees the picture on the wall. Disapproving...)* This back on is it?

MOLLY has one look at Saracen Bell then exits to see ARLENE. AARON watches her go. DOUGIE didn't like the patronising tone of LORENZO's last question. He looks at LORENZO coldly.

LORENZO: *(To MOLLY as she passes...)* Don't say anything to her.

AARON: Molly...

She blanks them all and exits. AARON seems a little less controlled now. MOLLY's resistance has rattled him a bit. That, and the fact he lost his temper.

DOUGIE, on the other hand, is focused – back on track and re-fuelled.

Pause.

LORENZO: Crazy thing is I like it. I know! I'm the only guy on Earth who *likes* the smell of smoke. I like it on other people. On their clothes. My parents didn't smoke see, so it reminds me of student parties and what I once thought of as, you know, worldliness. I could never do it. Tried once, for a play, but it just made me feel sick. She has no need to hide the fags. Does it for herself. *(Beat.)* Come on man, play nice. Everyone's getting...I could hear you all there, shouting. Switch it off. She'll be back.

There's a pause.

DOUGIE: Didnae know you were in a play Lorenzo.

LORENZO: Yeah, I was an actor. For a bit. Told you that, no?

DOUGIE: Aye? When was that again?

LORENZO: After Uni. In London. I was in an advert for the TSB.

DOUGIE: Big time!

LORENZO: *(Laughs weakly.)* Yeah.

DOUGIE: My God eh? Didnae know that. Thought it was a stand-up comic you were?

LORENZO: *(Beginning to feel a little uncomfortable.)* Yeah, well, I did that for a bit too. Same kind of era. I miss that actually. Quite a buzz. But then I re-trained as a chef, which was amazing. Similar rush: the stage in the spotlight and the heat of the pass with one hundred fifty covers on the board and counting. Bring it on. Ha!

DOUGIE: That when you did the cruise ships?

LORENZO: Yeah. Oh, I've done it all man.

DOUGIE: Ye huv as well.

LORENZO: Yeah. Life's a journey. Right? It all links in…the TV work into photography into web design into programming. I just…follow the trail, you know. Okay I might miss some aspects of certain professions, but I'm not a big one for reminiscing. *(The house.)* I have *this.* Know what I mean? Sometimes you have to make a small loss for a big gain.

DOUGIE: Aye. I'm the same.

LORENZO: Right.

DOUGIE: That's her type eh?

LORENZO: Mm?

DOUGIE: Must be. I mean it's no looks is it? We're pretty different looking. Ha ha ha!

LORENZO: Ha! I dunno. What you on about man?

DOUGIE: Well, we're drifters. Sure we are?

LORENZO: Em…

DOUGIE: Look, you do well and that. You've had some luck… somewhere…but you're drifting. Same as me. Jack of aw trades master of none. Dabble, dabble, dabble…see where you wash up next. I washed up in my old dear's box room! You washed up here. Worked out awright didn't it? It just must be what she likes.

LORENZO: She's right outside man.

DOUGIE: She likes being the one that sorts us out. That's what I think. Hard done by. That's Arlene. Cept she isnae. She gets exactly what she wants in the end. She got a kid out of me and she got cash out of you.

LORENZO: Dougie man, that's not cool. I'm taking the photo down now okay?

AARON: *(With bite.)* That's my computer.

LORENZO: And it's my projector. And my wall. So… *(he clicks the photo off)*…there you go.

Beat.

DOUGIE: *(Conspiratorially.)* Do you ever…you know…just like… "I'm the fucking man! Do as I fucking say!"? Just for kicks like?

LORENZO: Dougie…

DOUGIE: No? Never? Ooft. Try it. She goes nuts for that. Or she used to. I got her to shave her hair off.

AARON: No you didn't.

LORENZO: Okay…

DOUGIE: I did! Honest! Just told her…do it! Now! Right in the middle of…you know…in her mum and dad's bed. Right in the middle…she's like that "take control" or whatever! Just popped into my head!

AARON: Did you? Honestly?

DOUGIE: Aye! Her dad's shaver sitting on the hingme. Dressing table. I'm like that…"Shave! Now!". She loved it, man. I can totally picture her doing it too. Standing naked

55

at the mirror…with her dad's shaver…bzzzz…all off. *All* of it. Know what I mean?

AARON: No way.

DOUGIE: Aye. Everything. Oh man. She was wild in they days.

A pause as LORENZO levels his gaze at DOUGIE. He knows what's going on here…

LORENZO: Careful.

DOUGIE: Ever been a boxer, Lorenzo?

LORENZO: Careful.

DOUGIE: Ever punched someone in the face?

Pause.

DOUGIE takes something to eat, smiling. LORENZO looks off for ARLENE.

LORENZO: Look, if this whole thing is something you've dreamt up…

DOUGIE: Eh?

LORENZO: You and Aaron. In your horrible wee pub…

AARON: What you on about Lorenzo?

LORENZO: *(Cont.)* …Monday morning, man. I saw you going in. Half eleven on a bloody Monday. I was stopped at the lights. You were with some fat guy…

DOUGIE: Big Rydo.

LORENZO: You swore you wouldn't drink Aaron. Said you were done with all that.

AARON: *(The beer from earlier.)* Eh, you were the one pimping that on me two seconds ago.

LORENZO: I saw you. Huddled together like…bloody…witches round a cauldron…plotting. Probably. Monday morning.

DOUGIE's trying to keep a lid on his anger – the deal isn't sealed – but it's taking everything he's got…

DOUGIE: Think you've had one too many chocolate beers, son. Getting paranoid.

LORENZO: It'll pull everything down. Is what I'm saying. Honestly. She'll never let you near Molly again.

DOUGIE: Molly's an adult and I've dreamt nothing up.

LORENZO: Well then. I mean. Come on, man. You're an intelligent guy…

DOUGIE: Naw, I'm thick. Did you miss that bit?

LORENZO: *(Cont.)* …It must've crossed your mind that this is a con? A Nigerian prince, a pal trapped in jail in Morocco… it's one of those deals. You *know* that. Aaron, have you had a look at the page source or if there's a clue in the JavaScript or whatever?

AARON: I'm not into that stuff anymore.

LORENZO: *(Going to the laptop.)* Yeah, but you know what to do. You can usually tell if it's dodgy if the…

AARON slams the lid of the laptop down. Saracen disappears.

AARON: No. It's my computer.

A beat for a flicker of doubt to cross DOUGIE's mind. But he brushes it away easily…

He opens the laptop and presses return until the Saracen Bell picture comes on again.

DOUGIE: We'll let him look at the website. Eh, Aaron? Shut him up. *(To LORENZO.)* But I tell you something, I'll be wanting an apology from you in aw.

DOUGIE spins the laptop so LORENZO can get to it.

As LORENZO moves towards it…

AARON: It's easy to drift when there's money behind you.

LORENZO: Eh?

AARON: I said it's easier to drift through life when someone else is picking up the tab.

LORENZO: I've had a bit of luck.

AARON: Not really.

LORENZO turns away from the laptop to face AARON.

LORENZO: What?

AARON: You're not lucky. You haven't just had "luck". You were given it. Must be nice. To be given something. Rather than have it taken away.

DOUGIE smiles. He knows where AARON is going with this and is impressed...

DOUGIE: Aye! That's right. Aye! I mind you bought this place and you were saying you'd hingmed...you'd invented some kind of... *(To AARON)* what wis it?

AARON: Co-created an app.

DOUGIE: Aye. Co-created an app. And it had pure taken off and you'd got a load of money in one go an that. Thing is, we couldnae find that app. Could we?

AARON: Nope.

DOUGIE: So I asked Arlene and she told me straight out. No app. Your mum and dad had just given you the money. Right? But she asked me to play along. Save your pride an that. I get it. A man without pride isnae a man. And that can be hard for guys like us. We try. We fail. We drop it. Where's the pride in that, you know? Thing about her though, right... she's the opposite. She doesnae drop fuck all. She grips it! She's got you running back and forward to the kitchen and me on a chain. I'm a pet here and you're a waiter.

AARON: *(To LORENZO, miming a whip.)* Whccchhhht! *(Same to DOUGIE.)* Whccchhhht!

DOUGIE: Know what I mean? With me here...honestly...how can you ever win, man? You cannae. So instead you're scuttling about getting me fucking drinks. *(Closing the deal.)* Get her to sign the bank form. She'll hate me and I won't be round here as much. Talking about the good old days. Result, eh? Come on. Look out for number one. Prise her fingers from my chain. Get her to sign the form. Go on. Just fucking *tell* her to do it.

ARLENE and MOLLY come in. They stay on the far side of the room. MOLLY is upset. ARLENE looks defiant. She heard the last bit of that…

ARLENE: Doesnae matter if he tells me to do it. Doesnae matter if *you* tell me to do it. I can't do it.

DOUGIE: "*Won't* do it" ye mean. To keep me here, under glass…

ARLENE: No, I can't do it. I've just told Molly. Fair she knows. There's nothing more for her. Nothing more for anyone. Apart from what's in that account we don't have any other money.

Beat.

DOUGIE: Aye right.

ARLENE: It's true. There's no Plan B here. If you take that money she can't go to Uni. At all. End of. So that's that.

DOUGIE: Aye, nice try, Arlene, but Lorenzo's just offered us a blank cheque to drop the subject and behave. Should get your stories straight, eh?

ARLENE: Yeah well he doesn't know, does he? I do the finances.

AARON: I don't believe you.

ARLENE: Doesn't matter what you believe, Aaron.

AARON: So what about the match-funding?

ARLENE: The what?

AARON: The match funding! All those wee pep talks: "Come on, Aaron, apply for Uni and we'll match-fund any cash you have to borrow". That was just bullshit, was it? Or were you so sure it would never happen you didn't give it another thought?

ARLENE: We would've…

AARON: *(Cont.)* And anyway, she'll need more than twenty five grand, these days. Won't she? I mean, surely you must've planned for…?

ARLENE: *(Overlapping.)* We would've figured something out. Later on. That's what I'm saying. But for now – for her first year or so – that's all we've got.

DOUGIE: *(About LORENZO.)* Ask his mum and dad then. They've got it if you need it.

ARLENE: Not anymore. That door's shut.

LORENZO: Right, woah, woah…wait a minute, time out. Deep breath. *(To ARLENE.)* Doll, is this a…? Because you don't need to…you know…we can figure something out here as a family if we stay honest and true with each other and just remember that we're all…

ARLENE: *(Cutting him off.)* Jesus Christ, Lorenzo, it's not a fucking alibi. It's the truth. There is no more money. Not right now.

LORENZO: But…what about…?

ARLENE: It's gone. Question me later.

LORENZO: I thought you were saving and…?

ARLENE: *(Snapping at him, viciously.)* Were *you* saving? Or were you spending? Were you earning? Or were you racking up the debt as per? Do you have any idea how much debt we're in right this minute? To the bank? To your dad? *(To the room.)* Anyone? No. You haven't a clue. That's how come yous can all sleep at night and I'm wide awake. *(Back in LORENZO's face.)* So rather than asking why I haven't been saving my pennies and minding the house-keep like a good wee wifie, ask yourself about the role you play in this relationship. Not the traditional "man" that's for sure. Not much hunting and gathering going on in these parts is there? I put the bread on the table these days, so what's your department? Morale booster? Comedy sidekick?

That hits LORENZO hard.

LORENZO: Why are you…?

ARLENE: *(Still to LORENZO, goading…)* Do you know what you could do? If you actually wanted to be useful for once? You could get on that computer and find out for sure if they've made all this shit up. Is that something you think you could manage?

LORENZO: *(With a little bite.)* Actually I was already…and, yes, I know how to build a website Arlene, if that's what you mean. It was my bloody job after all.

ARLENE: So if The Journey Home Foundation was just Aaron in his room you could tell, right?

AARON: Don't touch that computer.

ARLENE: Something to hide?

DOUGIE: It's his.

ARLENE: Aye, and the money's hers! Is this getting through to you yet? If she doesn't have the money, she doesn't go to Uni. So we *can't* give you it. We can't. Are you that vicious, Dougie? Still?

Pause.

Then…

AARON: Sell the water feature then. If it's money you need. You know. You could do that. If your heart's set on Molly's further education then you could…I dunno…get the flat screen on eBay. You could cancel Sky Sports. Pawn the iPhone. Hawk your jewellery down the market. *(Getting bigger.)* The mixing decks in the garage can go as well, eh? Throw your Xbox and the HD projectors to the car booters and count your loot. Have you enough for her second year yet? No? Well. Flog the shelves of vinyl. And the Hi-fi System too. Punt the racks of designer gear. All those high heels and leather jackets must be worth a bomb, eh? Shop at Lidl to keep the costs down. Bye bye organic vegetables and fresh fruit, hello the fees for year three. Will you have the vim and vigour for an honours degree, I wonder, Molls? Not a problem if you do. They'll just sell the cameras and the car, no worries. And they'll sell the wine too. It's just sitting there, stacked up in the kitchen, undrunk. They'll sell the DVDs and the books and the Ikea furniture. They'll sell the whole joint, man. That's how much they care about you. They'll downsize in a heartbeat if that's what it takes. Right? They'll move into an ex-council on the old estate and we'll all be neighbours. A great big happy family. Waving our hankies…as lovely wee Molly flies off to the future. *(Beat. Then directly to ARLENE.)* It's not that you can't – I don't think – it's that you won't.

ARLENE holds his gaze for a beat or two then drops it. She allows the dust to settle in a big silence.

ARLENE takes a drink. Then…

ARLENE: Gave yourself away a wee bit there, eh Aaron?

AARON: Eh?

ARLENE: Aye. Gave yourself away. Spite. Hatred.

Pause.

AARON: *(Suddenly different.)* Fuck it. Just leave it then. Forget it. I dunno. *(To DOUGIE.)* Maybe just like…take some of it.

DOUGIE: Eh?

AARON: Just take some of it. Molly can have the rest. Fuck it. Fuck it.

DOUGLAS: What you on about? Naw. It's all or nothing. Has to be.

ARLENE: Why you coming at us though, Aaron? What you doing?

AARON: I'm trying to help Uncle Dougie make his point, that's what I'm doing. Or I was. But…

ARLENE: Trying to get some reparation?

AARON: *(Snapping.)* Yes! Actually.

ARLENE: And some revenge as well.

AARON: No…

ARLENE: And some money. Aye. Let's not forget that what you're really doing here is tricking us out of money.

AARON: No.

ARLENE: Oh I think so, aye. You want some money. For what though? What's the plan? You and your mum jet off to Africa for a lovely new life, problems left far behind? God, sometimes I forget that you're just a wee boy.

AARON: I'm not a wee boy.

ARLENE: If that's the plan then, aye, you are. Because that... this...is something an angry little kid would do. And even so...why you coming at us? *(DOUGIE.)* It's him... *(Cont.)*

LORENZO: We've always been bloody lovely to you, Aaron. An open door. You were loved here from day one.

ARLENE: *(Pointing at DOUGIE. Cont.)* ...He's the one to hate. Not us.

AARON: I said forget it! Just...let Molly have the cash. Okay? Forget it.

DOUGIE: *(To AARON.)* Eh? Naw, naw. What you on about, man? Naw, naw, naw...we went through this. Stick to the argument no matter what. Make them face the facts.

ARLENE: Face the facts? Oh my God! Right. Dougie. Here's the facts. Listening? *(Points at Saracen Bell.)* Aaron's made this all up.

AARON: I haven't.

DOUGIE: He hasnae.

ARLENE: He's stringing us along. He's stumbled on this Saracen Bell character somewhere, maybe surfing the web after *12 Years a Slave* and he's thought, "Ah ha. Here he is. Here's my chance". *(To DOUGIE.)* He's conning us. For money. And I think you know that. Don't you, Doogs? Deep down. Aye. And oh God...you must be shitting it. Cos what a fool you'll look then Douglas Bell. What a fucking fool.

DOUGIE: Naw. Way off. He wouldnae...no way. We're peas in a pod me and him. *(To AARON.)* Sure we are?

AARON: *(Small.)* Uh huh.

LORENZO: I just don't see why you'd be lashing out at us, Aaron. Because I tried with you man, I really did. I made you playlists. Taught you how to code.

DOUGIE: *(To LORENZO.)* You're nothing to him. I look after that boy.

ARLENE: Oh, is that right?

DOUGIE: Aye.

ARLENE: What, by taking him drinking? To the bookies? Turning him into a pathetic wee version of you?

DOUGIE: How am I…?

ARLENE: I saw it with my own eyes Dougie. He was here for three weeks and it was as clear as day: he was turning into you! Drunk and mumbling and resigned and angry. And worse. That look in his eye. That's you! I could see what was coming his way and I was not for having it! No way. He deserves better than you. He *is* better than you. So I told him.

DOUGIE: Told him what?

Beat.

MOLLY: Told him what?

ARLENE: And a fortnight later, here we are, with this. *(Saracen.)* But I *had* to tell him. I had to. It was my responsibility. As someone who genuinely cares for that boy I had to tell him.

MOLLY: Tell him what?

ARLENE: Molly doll…could you… *(give us a minute)*?

MOLLY: No! I'm staying, Mum. What did you tell him?

ARLENE: Molls just…

MOLLY: Oh my God! You treat me like a fucking baby!

LORENZO: Hey, hey…

MOLLY: Open your ears! This is all about me. All of it! The money and everything. Why has nobody clocked this? *I'm* the end of the family line. Not Dad. Not Aaron. Me. It should be my decision. My argument. My choice. Why are you saying Aaron made this all up? What did you tell him? What's going on?

AARON: Nothing.

MOLLY: I should know these things!

ARLENE: I don't want you to…

MOLLY: I thought we were free to talk about whatever we like in this house? God, we certainly hear enough about your sex life and your miraculous rise from the gutter, that's for sure. But when it comes to me, oh no – the shutters come down and baby's sent to the nursery. Well guess what, it goes both ways. Maybe I can't stand to hear any more about you or your troubles at work or how you had to struggle as a poor abused Catholic minority and all that kiddy on crap.

ARLENE: That wasn't kiddy on. Not where I lived.

AARON: It was. It is. It doesn't compare. It just doesn't. *(About MOLLY.)* She's right. With a gun to your head – "are you a Catholic or a Protestant?" – well, you can lie to save your life, right? Gun to my head, can I lie? Can I lie about what I am? No. It's incomparable. All that "I feel your pain" bullshit. Makes me sick.

ARLENE: *(To AARON.)* So you want me to tell her do you?

AARON doesn't know the answer to that. Part of him does, part of him doesn't. He's struggling to keep it together. He looks at the door. Should he just run? Or should he should just come out with it and be done?

MOLLY: I need to know what you're talking about. I deserve to know.

ARLENE: And do *you* want her to hear this, Dougie? Any thoughts?

DOUGIE: *(Unsure.)* She'll make the right choice. Know what I mean?

ARLENE: Aye, but do you know what *we* mean? Have you caught up with the conversation? Do you really want her to hear all this stuff? *(Pointing to AARON.)* About his dad? And you.

DOUGIE: *(About LORENZO, flapping a bit…)* If anyone's bloody going it should be him. This is none of his business anyway.

LORENZO: It's all my business! This is my family.

DOUGIE: No it's no.

LORENZO: Right, come on. What's going on Arlene? Aaron? Speak!

AARON: Saracen Bell is real…

ARLENE: Aaron's dad didn't just up and leave. He was threatened. He was attacked and told he could never come back… *(Cont.)*

MOLLY: What?

DOUGIE: Ach away you go.

ARLENE: *(To MOLLY. Cont.)* Your dad, Big Rydo and two or three of the other goons that he was knocking about with in those days, jumped Aaron's dad one Saturday night…

MOLLY: Dad's not a racist.

ARLENE: And that was that. *(To DOUGIE, about AARON.)* And he knows now. I told him, so you wouldn't be able to drag him down with you. He knows the truth. And that's why this is happening. All of this! *(Saracen.)* This is his revenge, Dougie! Because of that Saturday night. Open your eyes.

DOUGIE: *(Level. To ARLENE.)* Is that right? Okay. Fair enough. Except it didn't happen.

ARLENE: It did.

DOUGIE: It's a lie.

ARLENE: It's not.

MOLLY: Mum, dad is not a racist!

ARLENE: Where does he get his scratch cards from, Molly? The Pakis. What does he eat on a Friday night? A Chinky.

DOUGIE: And you said those things too. Everybody did.

ARLENE: Molly? Have you ever used those words?

MOLLY: *(Getting frightened.)* No, but…

ARLENE: No. Lorenzo, have you ever used those words?

LORENZO: *(Defeated and scowling.)* No.

DOUGIE: Aye but where I grew up…

ARLENE: I grew up where you grew up!

DOUGIE: And you said them in aw! I fucking remember you, Arlene Clarke.

ARLENE: Molly doesn't say those things cos she doesn't think them. She doesn't think them cos I raised her not to think them. Me! I did that. To drag her out of the murk. But what did you do? *(Saracen Bell.)* This!

DOUGIE: *(To ARLENE. Defiant.)* Cannae believe you. Lying about something like that.

ARLENE: Is it a lie that you called his dad "Black Bob". To his face. This was like, nineteen ninety five/ninety six by the way. Not sixty six, not seventy six, not eighty six...ninety six.

DOUGIE: Aye, but she's making it sound bloody...everybody called him that. He liked it. It was a... *(To AARON.)* He was a decent guy your Old Boy. Merchant Navy. He was a friend. Everybody thought he was ace. He jist couldnae be a dad.

ARLENE: When Bob walked down the street people would stop what they were doing and stare at him. Mouths hanging open. Nineteen...ninety...six.

DOUGIE: Aye but...jist cos...there wasnae that many...you didnae see...just cos you huvnae met different folk it doesnae mean you're racist. God sake.

ARLENE: Maybe not. But chasing him down the street...jumping him with a gang of guys...smashing his head off the road... holding a knife to his cock...that...yeah, *that* was racist.

DOUGIE: I didnae do that though. I just didnae do it.

ARLENE: Didn't you?

DOUGIE: Naw. Why would I do that? It's a lie. You're a liar. Imagine lying about that. There's an evil in you.

ARLENE: But I'm not lying. Am I?

Beat.

DOUGIE: *(To AARON and MOLLY.)* Well ask yourselves this, right...What kind of woman would want to be with a man capable of that kinda shit? Who would want to *stay* with him? After all of that. Get pregnant by him? After all of that.

(ARLENE.) This kind of woman? Her? I mean…why would she? Well…either it's not true. Or she was exactly the same.

ARLENE: Not *exactly* the same.

A silence.

MOLLY is reeling, trying to catch her breath. She's slipping from confusion to revulsion to anger…

AARON is staring at DOUGIE.

MOLLY: I didn't know…I didn't know that was even a… fucking… possibility.

There's a silence as she summons up the strength to look at them: her mother and father. She's thinking, "who are these people?"

Then…

LORENZO: People can change. You know. Remember that. We're none of us the same as we were when we were young.

DOUGIE: Didnae do it but. She's lying.

AARON: Just say sorry.

DOUGIE: I didnae do it Aaron! How can I say sorry if I didnae fucking…?!

AARON: *(Shouting.)* SAY SORRY!

DOUGIE: I didnae do anything.

Beat.

AARON: Black Guy Fucks Off From Family. That's all I had. A cliché. You gave me a cliché when I could've had something else…anything else…all those years…I could've had something that wasn't…empty.

DOUGIE: I didnae do anything!

AARON: And mum too. Who she is. That's on you. As well. Of course it is. It is.

DOUGIE: Eh? Naw, naw, naw…

AARON: Apologise!

DOUGIE: I didnae fucking do anything!

A big silence.

AARON: She's right by the way. There's no such thing as
The Journey Home Foundation. Me. That was me. Busted.
Bit embarrassing but…hey ho.

ARLENE: My God, Aaron, if money was so important to you…

AARON: *(Cutting her off.)* What? You'da given me some? You're
just after telling us there's none for me. There's plenty for
the Golden Girl but none for me! Same as it always was, eh?

Beat.

ARLENE: You're not my flesh and blood, son. I'm sorry, but
you're just not.

DOUGIE's struggling to process this…

DOUGIE: Naw, naw, naw…wait a minute…naw…that's…
you're just…no, I got an email…

AARON: *(To ARLENE about DOUGIE, unravelling.)* And it's his
money anyway. It is! No matter what you say. Which is…
cos he's the one that has to sting! It's his fault. Coulda been a
whole different story if it wasn't for him. Right? Coulda been
very different for me! So he has to pay. *(To DOUGIE.)* Say
sorry. Go on, man. Just say the words. Give us something to
move on from. Just something…

DOUGIE: Naw, you're off your nut, pal. You're as bad as your
bloody mum.

AARON: Don't you talk about her. Don't even talk about her!

DOUGIE: How? I'm her brother! And let me tell you
something – she was like that from day one. Nothing to do
with me. Day one: damaged goods. Sad, but there you go.
She shouldnae even've…she was bloody taken advantage
of! That was what was… *(To ARLENE, getting desperate…)*
This is you int it! You've done this. Bloody…spreading lies,
planting ideas in the boy's head.

ARLENE: Oh my God. Dougie…

DOUGIE: You made him do it.

ARLENE: How could I…?

DOUGIE: See the sacrifices I've made…

MOLLY: What sacrifices?

DOUGIE: And for Aaron too. I have. *(About ARLENE.)* She hasnae! She's sacrificed nothing.

ARLENE: Oh give it up Dougie, it's finished.

AARON: It's not. *(To DOUGIE.)* You have to say sorry.

DOUGIE spins to face AARON.

DOUGIE: *(Rage.)* I DON'T HAVE TO DO ANYTHING!

LORENZO: Right I think we all need to take a deep breath here…

MOLLY: I…I can't be here. I can't…

ARLENE: You stay put doll, it's them that's going.

DOUGIE: *(About ARLENE, with real anger…and fear.)* Look at her face. Bloody loving it. Aye, you're behind this alright. Fucking puppet master!

ARLENE: *(About DOUGIE.)* Aye here he is. I remember you.

DOUGIE: And I remember you. *(Points to Saracen Bell.)* There you're there! Eh? Eh?

ARLENE: What? Don't be so…

MOLLY: *(Rising…)* Can we please think about what we're actually going to do. Please. Because I feel like…

AARON: You have no…right…to…None of you. You don't have a say. You're nothing to me. You're just…some people.

DOUGIE: *(Looking at Saracen Bell.)* An anyway, he's real. And the slaves were real. An their kids were real. And I can help them. So. Nothing's changed. No really. It's the same. So it is. Keep going. We'll just keep going.

AARON makes a quick move for the door, to exit, but LORENZO grabs him – not forcibly, but AARON shoves him away roughly.

AARON: Get off me!

LORENZO: Right calm down. Okay? Everyone just calm down.

MOLLY: No.

MOLLY swipes a lamp to the floor smashing it.

LORENZO: Woh! Hey! No. Molly...

ARLENE: Molly you're bloody paying for that, I swear to God!

MOLLY: No I'm not. And I'm not calming down either. Calming down is just...it's the wrong move. Gets us nowhere. Aaron knows. Don't you Aaron? Staying in your room got you nowhere. So here we are instead! So what now? Smash it up? Right? That was it.

She picks up something else...a vase? An ornament?...and throws it to the floor violently...it smashes...

ARLENE: Molly! For Christ sake!

MOLLY: Knock the house down and walk away "clean". A firewall, a border and all that shit. Sounds good to me. Right Aaron? Is smashing it to smithereens still an option?

MOLLY chucks a pile of magazines to the floor...

She makes eye contact with AARON.

MOLLY: *(To AARON.)* Do you hate me?

AARON doesn't know the answer to that question. Or he can't bear the answer to that question. He's panting for breath, heart pounding...

He knocks a stack of books to the floor.

There's a beat and then MOLLY and AARON set about trashing the room.

They're not giddy or buzzing or having a laugh...they're focused. And each driven by a separate impulse.

Pillows, flowers, food, glasses, beer bottles...it all gets thrown to the floor. Pillows are ripped and scattered, tables are tipped.

ARLENE and LORENZO are rabbits in the headlights for a second or two, but they soon have to do something to stop the rampage. But it's futile. They're flapping and shouting...

DOUGIE watches greedily, but does nothing...

ARLENE: Molly! No! Stop it! You're being...this is unacceptable. Molly! Etc...

LORENZO: Right, you've made your point. Very good! We get it, but guys....No! Etc...

MOLLY is moving too fast and frantically to be stopped by ARLENE. So ARLENE gives up on restraint and attempts reverse psychology instead; standing by arms folded, unimpressed...

ARLENE: Oh, this is all very clever. How very insightful! This is modern political activism is it? Yes, how very articulate! And here was you not wanting to be treated like a baby. This is a tantrum that's all! You're being a baby! You're a child!

AARON goes to smash the projector. As he lifts it above his head the image of Saracen Bell is flung around the room, huge and distorted.

LORENZO: No! That's mine.

LORENZO tries to stop AARON, grabbing him awkwardly at first, but somehow managing to prevent him from throwing the projector. They're locked in a struggle...

LORENZO: Come on man! Stop! Dangerous! Jesus...

AARON: Let me go!

MOLLY: Let him go!

MOLLY tries to pull LORENZO off of AARON.

ARLENE: For fuck sake, Lorenzo...

LORENZO: No! Stop. Right. Come on.

AARON: Get off me!

LORENZO: Put it down!

AARON: Ah!

MOLLY: You're hurting him!

ARLENE: Lorenzo, just...take it off him for God sake just...

LORENZO: I'm trying! I...I can't...

ARLENE goes over and tries to prise MOLLY off of LORENZO but she can't get a grip.

The projector clatters to the floor. Saracen's face is projected, massively, onto the wall. The image is twisted, cracked.

And DOUGIE's just watching...waiting...far away.

ARLENE: Molly. Molly please for... *(Last resort.)* Fuck sake. Right, Dougie. Dougie! Come on, sort this out. Help us.

LORENZO: No! I can do it!

ARLENE: Dougie, help us here. I can't hold her.

LORENZO: I can fucking do it Arlene! Why do you have to...?

ARLENE: Dougie, come on. Now! Dougie help us!

LORENZO: I can do it.

ARLENE: Jesus Christ...

LORENZO: I CAN DO IT!

LORENZO pushes MOLLY off him violently. He grabs AARON around the neck and snaps his head back. AARON cries out in pain. LORENZO drags AARON back a few steps...

LORENZO: *(Still with his arm around AARON's throat. To ARLENE.)* If you would just let me...give me fucking space...to do what I need to do...without fucking...

AARON is choking. He struggles in a panic and somehow wriggles free of LORENZO's stranglehold. As he does his elbow catches LORENZO, painfully...

LORENZO: AAAHHH!

LORENZO snaps. He punches AARON hard in the face...once... twice...three times...

On the third punch AARON collapses to the floor, his face covered in blood.

MOLLY cries out and covers her mouth in shock.

AARON is on the floor, stunned and in pain.

ARLENE turns away and puts her head in her hands.

Not a thing from DOUGIE.

LORENZO: *(Raging. To DOUGIE.)* I want my fucking money back! All of it! I'll get lawyers. Fucking...

Big pause.

LORENZO is left panting for a beat or two as the adrenaline pounds through his system. But all his anger soon evaporates away to nothing.

All the violence has gone from the room.

LORENZO's scared now. He kneels beside AARON...

LORENZO: You okay buddy? You alright pal? That was a sore one, eh? You're okay. Em...we'll go to the hospital I think...

ARLENE: No. No.

LORENZO: But he's...

ARLENE: You'd be charged Lorenzo.

LORENZO: I did it though.

ARLENE: It would be my job.

Beat.

DOUGIE: It would. A vulnerable young boy attacked in a social worker's house? If the papers found out...oof. Messy. *(To LORENZO.)* You gonnie apologise for that, I wonder?

LORENZO: Yeah. *(To AARON.)* I'm...so sorry, man. I really am. I'm so, em, yeah, I dunno...I'm so sorry.

LORENZO tries to get down next to AARON to comfort him, wipe the blood from his face...but he's overcome. LORENZO covers his face to hide his tears. He weeps.

ARLENE can't look at LORENZO.

DOUGIE: No that it makes much difference, mind you.

AARON stands, panting for breath, wiping the blood from his face.

DOUGIE: Sign the bank form.

ARLENE: What?

DOUGIE: Sign the form and it goes no further. Aw this.

ARLENE: It's not real Dougie. There's no Journey Home Foundation or...

DOUGIE: Aye but there will be other ones. Real ones. In America or something. *(Saracen.)* Cos he's real. I can make up for all the bad that was done.

ARLENE: *(The room and the people in it.)* You could do that here.

DOUGIE: No. I couldnae. Sign the form. Or...know what I mean.

A beat.

ARLENE gets the bank form from wherever it is and signs it.

ARLENE: Was it worth it? Eh? Was it? All for one wee moment with the whip hand.

DOUGIE: I'm doing the right thing.

She comes over to DOUGIE and throws the form in his face. He picks it up.

AARON: Apologise.

DOUGIE: Still?

AARON: Apologise.

DOUGIE: No.

MOLLY: You can't even say "I'm sorry"?

DOUGIE: I *won't* say it.

MOLLY: So I'm not going to Uni?

DOUGIE: That's no my fault.

AARON: And I'm getting nothing?

DOUGIE: That's no my fault.

DOUGIE folds the bank form and puts it in his pocket. He heads for the door…

MOLLY: Hey, Dad?

DOUGIE turns to face MOLLY. She stands under the picture of Saracen Bell. She looks different…

MOLLY: That is a door of no return.

Beat.

DOUGIE: No it's no.

He turns, pushing past AARON, heading out the door…

Blackout.

THE END